150 DELICIOUS RECIPES FOR BUSY FAMILIES

Meredith® Print Advantage
Des Moines, Iowa

Meals in Minutes

Waterbury Publications, Inc.
Creative Director: Ken Carlson
Editorial Director: Lisa Kingsley

First Edition.

Printed in the United States of America.
ISBN: 978-0-696-30071-4

All of us at Meredith Print Advantage are dedicated to providing you information and ideas to enhance your home. We welcome your comments and suggestions. Write to us at: Meredith Print Advantage, 1716 Locust St., Des Moines, IA 50309-3023.

Pictured on cover:
Pronto Pasta, recipe on page 135

CONTENTS

DINNER IS BACK!

Between Monday night soccer practice and Wednesday night ballet lessons, family life can be very hectic—sometimes even a little frantic! After working all day, driving the kids around, and running all your errands, finding time to whip together a home-cooked meal may seem like a daunting task. But stop and take a deep breath.

Meals at home are possible. No matter how much or how little time you have to put good food on the table for your family, there's a recipe here for you. You'll find three main-dish sections in this book, each tailor-made to fit your time constraints. The first section includes the quickest recipes ever—ready in 20 minutes or less. The second section keeps it simple with meals that can be created in 30 minutes. And the third section gives you 40-plus 40-minute options for when you have a little more time.

Meals in Minutes is designed just for you—the time-crunched grown-ups who are juggling everything but also know the importance of home-cooked meals for themselves and their families. These recipes were designed to be not only irresistible but also healthful and super-convenient to prepare. So go ahead—enjoy dinner again!

STOCKING THE PANTRY

Each of the recipes includes a shopping list and a pantry list. The former are things you might need to pick up at the grocery store, while the latter includes items you probably have in your kitchen. Before you start, here are the absolute basics you should keep on hand—with them, dinner is never far away!

ESSENTIAL PANTRY FOODS

All-purpose flour
Baking powder and soda
Balsamic vinegar
Barbecue sauce
Bottled hot pepper sauce
Bottled salad dressing (Italian, ranch)
Bread
Cayenne pepper
Chili powder
Cider vinegar
Cornstarch
Crushed red pepper
Dried basil
Dried Italian seasoning
Dried oregano
Dried pasta (spaghetti, angel hair, elbow macaroni, orzo, small shell macaroni)
Dried thyme
Fine dry bread crumbs
Garlic bulbs or bottled minced garlic
Garlic salt
Ground black pepper
Ground cinnamon
Ground cumin
Honey
Ketchup
Maple syrup
Mayonnaise (light or regular)

Mustard (Dijon-style and yellow)
Nonstick cooking spray
Oil (cooking, olive, vegetable)
Peanut butter
Rice (white and brown)
Salt
Shortening
Soy sauce
Sugar (granulated and brown)
Worcestershire sauce

ESSENTIAL REFRIGERATOR ITEMS

Butter (margarine)
Eggs
Milk
Orange juice

Once the basics are tucked away in your cupboards, stock up on some other commonly used foods. Mix and match from each category and you'll never be without dinner again!

OTHER PANTRY FOODS

Canned beans
Canned chicken, beef, and vegetable broth
Canned coconut milk
Canned diced tomatoes
Canned soup
Canned tuna or salmon
Corn muffin mix
Curry powder
Dried egg or ramen noodles
Flour or corn tortillas
Instant rice (white or brown)
Jars of gravy
Jelly and/or jams
Nuts (peanuts, almonds, walnuts)
Panko (Japanese-style bread crumbs)
Pasta sauce
Pesto
Pickles
Pizza sauce
Pouches of cooked rice
Quick-cooking couscous
Salsa
Stewed tomatoes (plain, Mexican-style, Italian-style)
Stir-fry or hoisin sauce

OTHER REFRIGERATOR AND FREEZER ITEMS

Beef stir-fry strips
Cheese (cheddar, feta, Parmesan)
Chicken breasts
Cream cheese and flavored cream cheese spreads
Dairy sour cream
Deli meats (ham, roast beef, turkey)
Frozen bread or bread dough
Frozen vegetables
Ground beef
Plain yogurt
Pork chops
Refrigerated pasta
Shredded cheese
Sliced bacon
Sliced cheese

OTHER PRODUCE

Broccoli
Carrots
Celery
Cucumbers
Green beans
Mixed salad greens packages
Mushrooms
Onions
Potatoes
Shredded cabbage with carrot (coleslaw mix)
Sweet peppers
Sweet potatoes
Yellow summer squash
Zucchini

ASIAN PORK SOUP, page 46

MEALS

20
MINUTES

QUICK THAI CHICKEN

START TO FINISH: *20 minutes*

- **4 skinless, boneless chicken breast halves**
- **1 tablespoon cooking oil**
- **¾ cup unsweetened coconut milk**
- **¼ cup peanut butter**
- **¼ teaspoon ground ginger**
- **¼ teaspoon ground black pepper**
- **4 green onions, cut into 1-inch pieces**
- **¼ cup honey-roasted peanuts, coarsely chopped**

1. In a large skillet cook chicken in hot oil over medium heat for 8 to 12 minutes or until no longer pink (170°F), turning occasionally to brown evenly. Remove chicken from skillet; cover to keep warm.

2. In a small bowl whisk together coconut milk, peanut butter, ginger, and pepper; set aside. Add green onions to skillet. Cook and stir about 2 minutes or until tender. Stir in coconut milk mixture. Cook and stir until bubbly. Spoon over chicken; sprinkle with peanuts.

Makes 4 servings

PER SERVING: 415 cal., 25 g total fat (11 g sat. fat), 82 mg chol., 192 mg sodium, 8 g carbo., 2 g fiber, 39 g pro.

SHOPPING LIST

4 skinless, boneless chicken breast halves
1 14-ounce can unsweetened coconut milk
1 8-ounce jar peanut butter
1 small container ground ginger
1 bunch green onions
1 8-ounce container honey-roasted peanuts

PANTRY LIST

Cooking oil
Ground black pepper

20
MINUTES

CHICKEN VERONIQUE

START TO FINISH: *20 minutes*

- **4 skinless, boneless chicken breast halves**
- **¼ teaspoon salt**
- **¼ teaspoon ground black pepper**
- **¼ cup butter**
- **1 cup seedless red grapes, halved**
- **3 tablespoons sherry vinegar or red wine vinegar**
- **¼ teaspoon dried thyme, crushed**

1. Sprinkle chicken with salt and pepper. In a large skillet cook chicken in 2 tablespoons of the hot butter over medium-high heat for 8 to 10 minutes or until no longer pink (170°F), turning once. Transfer to a serving platter; keep warm.

2. For sauce, add the remaining 2 tablespoons butter, grapes, vinegar, and thyme to the hot skillet. Cook and stir until slightly thick, loosening any brown bits on bottom of skillet. Serve sauce over chicken.

Makes 4 servings

PER SERVING: 301 cal., 15 g total fat (8 g sat. fat), 115 mg chol., 348 mg sodium, 7 g carbo., 0 g fiber, 33 g pro.

SHOPPING LIST

4 skinless, boneless chicken breast halves

1 small bag seedless red grapes

1 small bottle sherry vinegar

PANTRY LIST

Salt

Ground black pepper

Butter

Dried thyme

20
MINUTES

HAWAIIAN SWEET AND SOUR CHICKEN

START TO FINISH: *20 minutes*

- **2 tablespoons slivered almonds**
- **1 tablespoon cooking oil**
- **1 medium carrot, thinly bias-sliced**
- **1 medium green sweet pepper, cut into bite-size strips**
- **4 green onions, bias-sliced**
- **12 ounces chicken breast tenderloins, halved crosswise**
- **1 8- to 10-ounce bottle sweet and sour sauce**
- **1 8-ounce can pineapple chunks (juice pack), drained**
- **1 8.8-ounce pouch cooked long grain rice**

SHOPPING LIST

1 2-ounce package slivered almonds
1 1-pound package carrots
1 medium green sweet pepper
1 bunch green onions
12 ounces chicken breast tenderloins
1 8- to 10-ounce bottle sweet and sour sauce
1 8-ounce can pineapple chunks (juice pack)
1 8.8-ounce pouch cooked long grain rice

PANTRY LIST

Cooking oil

1. Preheat oven to 350°F. Spread almonds in a single layer in a shallow baking pan. Bake for 5 to 10 minutes or until golden brown, stirring once or twice; set aside.

2. Meanwhile, heat oil in a wok or large skillet over medium-high heat. Add carrot; cook and stir for 2 minutes. Add sweet pepper; cook and stir for 2 minutes. Add green onions; cook and stir for 1 minute more or until vegetables are crisp-tender. Remove vegetables from skillet.

3. Add chicken to hot wok (add more oil if needed). Cook and stir for 3 to 4 minutes or until chicken is no longer pink. Return vegetables to wok. Add sweet and sour sauce and drained pineapple. Heat through.

4. Prepare rice according to package directions. Serve chicken mixture with rice; top with toasted almonds.

Makes 4 servings

PER SERVING: 390 cal., 8 g total fat (1 g sat. fat), 49 mg chol., 263 mg sodium, 51 g carbo., 3 g fiber, 23 g pro.

20
MINUTES

LEMON-TARRAGON CHICKEN TOSS

START TO FINISH: *20 minutes*

- **6 ounces dried fettuccine or linguine**
- **2 cups broccoli or cauliflower florets**
- **½ cup reduced-sodium chicken broth**
- **3 tablespoons lemon juice**
- **1 tablespoon honey**
- **2 teaspoons cornstarch**
- **¼ teaspoon ground white pepper**
- **12 ounces skinless, boneless chicken breasts, cut into bite-size strips**
- **2 teaspoons olive oil or cooking oil**
- **½ cup shredded carrot**
- **1 tablespoon snipped fresh tarragon or ½ teaspoon dried tarragon, crushed**
- **Lemon slices, halved (optional)**

1. Cook pasta according to package directions, adding broccoli during the last 4 minutes of cooking. Drain.

2. Meanwhile, in a small bowl combine broth, lemon juice, honey, cornstarch, and white pepper; set aside.

3. In a large nonstick skillet cook and stir chicken in hot oil for 3 to 4 minutes or until no longer pink. Stir cornstarch mixture; add to skillet. Cook and stir until thick and bubbly. Add carrot and tarragon; cook for 1 minute more.

4. To serve, spoon chicken mixture over pasta. If desired, garnish with lemon slices.

Makes 4 servings

PER SERVING: 320 cal., 4 g total fat (1 g sat. fat), 49 mg chol., 143 mg sodium, 43 g carbo., 3 g fiber, 27 g pro.

SHOPPING LIST

1 8-ounce package dried fettuccine

1 head fresh broccoli

1 14-ounce container reduced-sodium chicken broth

1 lemon

1 small container ground white pepper

12 ounces boneless, skinless chicken breasts

1 small package shredded carrot

1 small package fresh tarragon

PANTRY LIST

Honey

Cornstarch

Olive oil

20
MINUTES

CARIBBEAN CHICKEN

START TO FINISH: *20 minutes*

- **1½ cups quick-cooking brown rice**
- **1 pound chicken breast tenderloins**
- **¼ teaspoon salt**
- **⅛ to ¼ teaspoon cayenne pepper**
- **1 teaspoon roasted peanut oil or cooking oil**
- **1 medium sweet potato, peeled, halved lengthwise, and thinly sliced**
- **1 small banana pepper, seeded and chopped**
- **¾ cup unsweetened pineapple juice**
- **1 teaspoon cornstarch**
- **2 unripe bananas, quartered lengthwise and cut into ¾-inch pieces**

1. Prepare rice according to package directions.

2. Meanwhile, season chicken with salt and cayenne pepper. In a large skillet cook chicken in hot oil over medium heat for 3 to 4 minutes or until brown, turning once. Add sweet potato slices and banana pepper. Cook and stir for 5 to 6 minutes more.

3. In a small bowl stir together unsweetened pineapple juice and cornstarch. Add to skillet. Cook, stirring gently, until bubbly. Add banana pieces. Cook and stir for 2 minutes more. Serve over rice.

Makes 4 servings

PER SERVING: 335 cal., 4 g total fat (1 g sat. fat), 66 mg chol., 244 mg sodium, 47 g carbo., 5 g fiber, 30 g pro.

SHOPPING LIST

1 8-ounce package quick-cooking brown rice

1 pound chicken breast tenderloins

1 small bottle roasted peanut oil

1 medium sweet potato

1 small banana pepper

1 6-ounce can unsweetened pineapple juice

2 unripe bananas

PANTRY LIST

Salt

Cayenne pepper

Cornstarch

20
MINUTES

STIR-FRY CHICKEN AND RICE

START TO FINISH: *10 minutes*

- ½ **cup frozen peas**
- 1 **8.8-ounce pouch cooked brown or white rice**
- 1 **pound chicken breast tenderloins, halved crosswise**
- 1 **tablespoon cooking oil**
- ¼ **cup bottled stir-fry sauce**
- 1 **2-ounce package oven-roasted sliced almonds**

1. Stir peas into rice pouch. Heat in microwave according to package directions.

2. Meanwhile, in a large skillet cook and stir chicken in hot oil over medium-high heat for 2 to 3 minutes or until no longer pink. Stir rice mixture into skillet. Stir in stir-fry sauce; heat through. Sprinkle with almonds.

Makes 4 servings

PER SERVING: 311 cal., 9 g total fat (1 g sat. fat), 66 mg chol., 453 mg sodium, 25 g carbo., 2 g fiber, 31 g pro.

SHOPPING LIST

1 8.8-ounce pouch cooked brown rice
1 10-ounce package frozen peas
1 pound chicken breast tenders
1 8-ounce bottle stir-fry sauce
1 2-ounce package oven-roasted sliced almonds

PANTRY LIST

Cooking oil

20
MINUTES

SOUTHERN CHICKEN SALAD

START TO FINISH: *20 minutes*

- ½ **cup dairy sour cream**
- ¼ **cup white wine vinegar**
- 3 **to 4 tablespoons Dijon-style mustard**
- 2 **cloves garlic, minced**
- ½ **teaspoon salt**
- ¼ **teaspoon ground black pepper**
- 6 **cups torn mixed salad greens**
- ½ **cup lightly packed small fresh mint leaves**
- 2 **tablespoons shredded fresh basil or marjoram leaves**
- 4 **slices Texas toast or large slices sourdough bread, toasted**
- 2 **to 4 tablespoons honey butter**
- 1 **purchased roasted chicken, quartered***
- 4 **medium peaches or nectarines, pitted and sliced**

1. For dressing, in a small bowl whisk together sour cream, vinegar, mustard, garlic, salt, and pepper; set aside.

2. In a large bowl toss together greens, mint, and basil. Spread each toast slice with honey butter and place 1 slice on each of 4 plates. Top each with some of the greens. Arrange chicken and peaches on top of greens. Drizzle with dressing.

Makes 4 servings

PER SERVING: 677 cal., 36 g total fat (13 g sat. fat), 218 mg chol., 965 mg sodium, 37 g carbo., 3 g fiber, 52 g pro.

*Note: Chicken can be warm or chilled.

SHOPPING LIST

1 8-ounce carton dairy sour cream
1 bottle white wine vinegar
1 7-ounce package mixed salad greens
1 package fresh mint
1 small package fresh basil
4 slices Texas toast
1 small container honey butter
1 purchased roasted chicken
4 medium peaches
1 bulb garlic

PANTRY LIST

Dijon-style mustard
Salt
Ground black pepper

20
MINUTES

SOUTHWESTERN COBB SALAD

START TO FINISH: *20 minutes*

- **1 10-ounce package chopped hearts of romaine**
- **1 6-ounce package refrigerated cooked Southwestern chicken breast strips**
- **1 15-ounce can black beans, rinsed and drained**
- **1 cup halved grape or cherry tomatoes**
- **1 cup lime-flavor or plain tortilla chips, coarsely broken (about 1 ounce)**
- **2 medium avocados, peeled, seeded, and sliced**
- **1 11-ounce can whole kernel corn with sweet peppers, drained**
- **½ cup shredded Mexican-style four-cheese blend**
- **½ cup thinly sliced red onion**
- **½ cup bottled spicy ranch salad dressing***

1. Spread romaine on a large serving platter. Arrange chicken, beans, tomatoes, tortilla chips, sliced avocados, corn, cheese, and onion in rows over the lettuce. Serve with dressing.

Makes 6 servings

PER SERVING: 363 cal., 22 g total fat (5 g sat. fat), 33 mg chol., 880 mg sodium, 32 g carbo., 9 g fiber, 17 g pro.

***Test Kitchen Tip:** If you can't find spicy ranch salad dressing, mix ½ cup ranch salad dressing with 2 tablespoons barbecue sauce.

SHOPPING LIST

1 10-ounce package chopped hearts of romaine
1 6-ounce package refrigerated cooked Southwestern chicken breast strips
1 15-ounce can black beans
1 pint grape tomatoes
1 13-ounce bag lime-flavor tortilla chips
2 medium avocados
1 11-ounce can whole kernel corn with sweet peppers
1 8-ounce package shredded Mexican-style four-cheese blend
1 small red onion
1 16-ounce bottle spicy ranch salad dressing

20
MINUTES

DILL CHICKEN WRAPS

START TO FINISH: *20 minutes*

- **4 10-inch flour tortillas**
- **¼ cup dairy sour cream dill-flavor dip**
- **½ cup fresh spinach leaves**
- **8 ounces sliced cooked chicken breast**
- **2 dill pickle spears, quartered lengthwise**
- **4 ounces smoked Gouda or mozzarella cheese, shredded (1 cup)**

1. Wrap tortillas in plain white paper towels. Microwave on 100% power (high) for 1 minute.

2. Spread each tortilla with 1 tablespoon of the dip. Top with spinach leaves and chicken. Arrange pickle spears lengthwise down the center of each tortilla; sprinkle with cheese.

3. Tightly roll up tortillas; secure with wooden picks, if necessary. If desired, cut rolls in half.

Makes 4 wraps

PER WRAP: 363 cal., 16 g total fat (8 g sat. fat), 88 mg chol., 666 mg sodium, 24 g carbo., 1 g fiber, 28 g pro.

SHOPPING LIST

1 14-ounce package flour tortillas
1 8-ounce container dairy sour cream dill-flavor dip
1 5-ounce package fresh spinach
8 ounces sliced smoked cooked chicken breast
4 ounces smoked Gouda cheese
1 16-ounce jar dill pickle spears

20 MINUTES

WASATCH MOUNTAIN CHILI

START TO FINISH: *15 minutes*

- **1 medium onion, chopped (½ cup)**
- **1 tablespoon cooking oil**
- **1 15- to 16-ounce can hominy, drained**
- **1 15- to 16-ounce can Great Northern beans, rinsed and drained**
- **1 14-ounce can reduced-sodium chicken broth**
- **1 9-ounce package frozen cooked chicken breast strips**
- **¼ cup lime juice**
- **2 tablespoons chopped fresh cilantro**
- **¼ teaspoon ground cumin**
- **¼ teaspoon ground black pepper**
- **½ cup shredded Colby and Monterey Jack cheese, Monterey Jack, or cheddar cheese (2 ounces)**
- **Bottled green salsa (optional)**
- **White corn tortilla chips (optional)**
- **Fresh cilantro leaves (optional)**

1. In a large saucepan cook onion in hot oil over medium heat for 3 minutes. Stir in hominy, beans, chicken broth, frozen chicken, lime juice, cilantro, cumin, and pepper. Cover and bring to boiling over high heat, stirring occasionally. Serve topped with cheese and, if desired, salsa, tortilla chips, and fresh cilantro.

Makes 4 servings

PER SERVING: 434 cal., 14 g total fat (5 g sat. fat), 58 mg chol., 1,001 mg sodium, 48 g carbo., 9 g fiber, 31 g pro.

SHOPPING LIST

1 medium onion
1 15-ounce can hominy
1 15-ounce can Great Northern beans
1 14-ounce can reduced-sodium chicken broth
1 9-ounce package frozen cooked chicken breast strips
1 small bottle lime juice
1 bunch fresh cilantro
1 small container ground cumin
1 8-ounce package shredded Colby and Monterey Jack cheese

PANTRY LIST

Cooking oil
Ground black pepper

20
MINUTES

CAJUN CHICKEN TORTELLINI

START TO FINISH: *20 minutes*

- 1 **20-ounce package refrigerated three-cheese tortellini**
- 1 **small red onion, cut into thin wedges**
- 1 **medium yellow sweet pepper, cut into bite-size strips**
- 1 **tablespoon olive oil**
- 2 **6-ounce packages refrigerated cooked chicken breast strips**
- 1 **10-ounce container refrigerated Alfredo pasta sauce**
- 1 **teaspoon Cajun seasoning**

1. Prepare tortellini according to package directions; drain and return to pan.

2. Meanwhile, in a large skillet cook onion and sweet pepper in hot oil over medium heat for 5 to 7 minutes or until tender, stirring occasionally. Stir in chicken, pasta sauce, and Cajun seasoning. Heat through. Add to tortellini; toss to coat.

Makes 6 servings

PER SERVING: 574 cal., 22 g total fat (19 g sat. fat), 109 mg chol., 1,417 mg sodium, 64 g carbo., 4 g fiber, 43 g pro.

SHOPPING LIST

1 20-ounce package refrigerated three-cheese tortellini

1 small red onion

1 medium yellow sweet pepper

2 6-ounce packages refrigerated cooked chicken breast strips

1 10-ounce container refrigerated Alfredo pasta sauce

1 small jar Cajun seasoning

PANTRY LIST

Olive oil

20 MINUTES

CHICKEN TENDERS PARMESAN

START TO FINISH: *20 minutes*

- **1 12-ounce package frozen cooked breaded chicken breast tenders**
- **1 cup bottled marinara sauce**
- **½ cup shredded Italian cheese blend**
- **2 tablespoons snipped fresh basil (optional)**

1. Preheat oven to 425°F. Place chicken tenders in a 2-quart square baking dish. Top with marinara sauce and cheese. Bake for 15 minutes or until hot and bubbly. If desired, sprinkle with fresh basil.

Makes 4 servings

PER SERVING: 279 cal., 14 g total fat (4 g sat. fat), 35 mg chol., 863 mg sodium, 23 g carbo., 2 g fiber, 17 g pro.

SHOPPING LIST

1 12-ounce package frozen cooked breaded chicken breast tenders

1 26-ounce jar marinara sauce

1 8-ounce package shredded Italian cheese blend

1 bunch fresh basil

20
MINUTES

HONEY-CRANBERRY TURKEY

START TO FINISH: *20 minutes*

- **2 turkey breast tenderloins, halved horizontally (about 1¼ pounds)**
- **Salt and ground black pepper**
- **1 tablespoon butter**
- **½ cup whole cranberry sauce**
- **1 tablespoon honey**
- **½ teaspoon finely shredded lemon peel**
- **1 tablespoon lemon juice**

1. Sprinkle turkey with salt and pepper. In a very large skillet cook turkey in hot butter over medium-high heat for 12 to 15 minutes or until no longer pink (170°F), turning once. Transfer to a serving platter; reserve drippings in skillet. Cover turkey to keep warm.

2. Stir cranberry sauce, honey, lemon peel, and lemon juice into reserved drippings in skillet. Cook and stir until heated through. Spoon over turkey.

Makes 4 servings

PER SERVING: 252 cal., 4 g total fat (2 g sat. fat), 96 mg chol., 246 mg sodium, 18 g carbo., 0 g fiber, 35 g pro.

SHOPPING LIST
2 turkey breast tenderloins
1 16-ounce can whole cranberry sauce
1 lemon

PANTRY LIST
Salt
Ground black pepper
Butter
Honey

20
MINUTES

ITALIAN TURKEY BURGERS

START TO FINISH: *20 minutes*

- **1 pound uncooked ground turkey**
- **2 teaspoons dried Italian seasoning, crushed**
- **½ cup shredded mozzarella cheese (2 ounces)**
- **¼ cup mayonnaise or salad dressing**
- **2 tablespoons refrigerated basil pesto**
- **4 hamburger buns, split and toasted if desired**
- **1 small tomato, thinly sliced**

SHOPPING LIST

1 pound uncooked ground turkey

1 8-ounce package shredded mozzarella cheese

1 7-ounce container refrigerated basil pesto

1 package hamburger buns

1 small tomato

PANTRY LIST

Italian seasoning

Mayonnaise

1. In a medium bowl combine ground turkey and Italian seasoning. Shape into four ½-inch-thick patties (use wet hands if necessary). Lightly grease the rack of an indoor electric grill or grill pan. Preheat grill or grill pan. Place patties on the grill rack or in pan. If using a grill with a cover, close the lid. Grill for 5 to 7 minutes for a covered grill or 9 to 12 minutes for an uncovered grill or grill pan, turning once, or until no longer pink (165°F). Remove burgers to a plate. Top hot burgers with cheese and let stand, covered with foil, for 1 to 2 minutes or until cheese melts.

2. Meanwhile, in a small bowl combine mayonnaise and pesto. Spread mixture on cut sides of hamburger buns. Top bun bottoms with turkey burgers and sliced tomatoes. Add bun tops.

Makes 4 servings

PER SERVING: 467 cal., 28 g total fat (7 g sat. fat), 106 mg chol., 550 mg sodium, 24 g carbo., 1 g fiber, 29 g pro.

20
MINUTES

TURKEY CHILI WITH A TWIST

START TO FINISH: *20 minutes*

- **12 ounces uncooked bulk turkey Italian sausage or uncooked ground turkey**
- **2 15-ounce cans chili beans with chili gravy**
- **1 cup bottled salsa with lime**
- **1 15-ounce can golden hominy, drained**
- **⅔ cup water**
- **⅓ cup sliced green onions**

1. In a large saucepan cook turkey sausage until brown. Stir in undrained chili beans, salsa, hominy, and the water. Heat through. Sprinkle with green onions.

Makes 4 to 5 servings

PER SERVING: 470 cal., 11 g total fat (3 g sat. fat), 45 mg chol., 1,897 mg sodium, 64 g carbo., 16 g fiber, 28 g pro.

SHOPPING LIST

12 ounces uncooked bulk turkey Italian sausage

2 15-ounce cans chili beans with chili gravy

1 8-ounce jar salsa

1 15-ounce can golden hominy

1 bunch green onions

20
MINUTES

HERB-HORSERADISH STEAKS

START TO FINISH: *20 minutes*

2 12- to 14-ounce beef top loin steaks, cut 1 inch thick

Salt and ground black pepper

2 tablespoons prepared horseradish

1 tablespoon Dijon-style mustard

2 teaspoons snipped fresh (flat-leaf) parsley

1 teaspoon snipped fresh thyme

Broiled cherry tomatoes (optional)

Broiled sweet pepper strips (optional)

1. Preheat broiler. Season steaks with salt and pepper. Place steaks on the unheated rack of a broiler pan. Broil 4 inches from heat for 7 minutes. Meanwhile, combine horseradish, mustard, parsley, and thyme.

2. Turn steaks. Broil for 8 to 9 minutes more for medium doneness (160°F). The last 1 minute of broiling, spread steaks with horseradish mixture. If desired, serve with tomatoes and peppers.

Makes 4 servings

PER SERVING: 284 cal., 15 g total fat (6 g sat. fat), 84 mg chol., 351 mg sodium, 1 g carbo., 0 g fiber, 33 g pro.

Test Kitchen Tip: Steaks also may be grilled directly over medium coals for the same amount of time.

SHOPPING LIST

2 12-ounce beef top loin steaks

1 8-ounce bottle prepared horseradish sauce

1 bunch fresh (flat-leaf) parsley

1 package fresh thyme

PANTRY LIST

Salt

Ground black pepper

Dijon-style mustard

20
MINUTES

TOMATO-HERB STEAK

START TO FINISH: *20 minutes*

- **2 beef top loin steaks, cut ¾ inch thick**
- **Salt and ground black pepper**
- **Nonstick cooking spray**
- **½ cup sliced green onions**
- **2 teaspoons snipped fresh basil or 1 teaspoon dried basil, crushed**
- **1 cup chopped tomato**

1. Cut steaks in half; season with salt and pepper. Lightly coat a large heavy skillet with cooking spray. Heat skillet over medium-high heat. Add steaks and reduce heat to medium; cook for 5 to 10 minutes or to desired doneness (145°F for medium-rare or 160°F for medium), turning once. Remove steaks and keep warm.

2. Add green onions and dried basil (if using) to drippings in skillet. Cook about 2 minutes or until onions are tender. Stir in tomato and fresh basil (if using). Serve over steaks. Sprinkle lightly with salt.

Makes 4 servings

PER SERVING: 219 cal., 11 g total fat (4 g sat. fat), 66 mg chol., 207 mg sodium, 3 g carbo., 1 g fiber, 26 g pro.

SHOPPING LIST

2 beef top loin steaks
1 bunch green onions
1 package fresh basil
1 large tomato

PANTRY LIST

Salt
Ground black pepper
Nonstick cooking spray

20
MINUTES

BEEF-BROCCOLI NOODLE BOWL

START TO FINISH: *20 minutes*

- **8 ounces packaged beef stir-fry strips**
- **1 tablespoon cooking oil**
- **2 teaspoons grated fresh ginger or bottled minced ginger**
- **3 cloves garlic, minced**
- **2 14-ounce cans beef broth**
- **2 tablespoons reduced-sodium soy sauce**
- **2 teaspoons rice vinegar**
- **2 cups broccoli florets**
- **1½ cups packaged fresh julienne carrots**
- **1 3-ounce package ramen noodles (any flavor)**

1. In a large saucepan cook beef strips in hot oil until brown. Stir in ginger and garlic; cook 1 minute more. Add beef broth, soy sauce, and vinegar. Bring to boiling; reduce heat. Add broccoli and carrots. Simmer, covered, for 3 minutes or until crisp-tender. Break ramen noodles into smaller pieces (discard spice packet). Add noodles to saucepan. Simmer, uncovered, for 3 minutes or until noodles and vegetables are tender.

Makes 4 servings

PER SERVING: 262 cal., 11 g total fat (1 g sat. fat), 24 mg chol., 1,066 mg sodium, 22 g carbo., 3 g fiber, 19 g pro.

SHOPPING LIST

1 8-ounce package beef stir-fry strips
1 piece fresh ginger
2 14-ounce cans beef broth
1 10-ounce bottle reduced-sodium soy sauce
1 10-ounce bottle rice vinegar
1 bunch broccoli
1 10-ounce package fresh julienne carrots
1 3-ounce package ramen noodles

PANTRY LIST

Cooking oil
Garlic

20
MINUTES

BEEF-VEGETABLE STEW

START TO FINISH: *20 minutes*

- **2 cups water**
- **1 10.75-ounce can condensed golden mushroom soup**
- **1 10.75-ounce can condensed tomato soup**
- **½ cup dry red wine or beef broth**
- **2 cups chopped cooked roast beef**
- **1 16-ounce package frozen sugar snap stir-fry vegetables or one 16-ounce package frozen cut broccoli**
- **½ teaspoon dried thyme, crushed**

1. In a 4-quart Dutch oven combine the water, mushroom soup, tomato soup, and wine. Stir in beef, frozen vegetables, and thyme.

2. Cook over medium heat until bubbly, stirring frequently. Continue cooking, uncovered, for 4 to 5 minutes or until vegetables are crisp-tender, stirring occasionally.

Makes 5 servings

PER SERVING: 304 cal., 10 g total fat (4 g sat. fat), 56 mg chol., 852 mg sodium, 24 g carbo., 4 g fiber, 23 g pro.

SHOPPING LIST

1 10.75-ounce can condensed golden mushroom soup

1 10.75-ounce can condensed tomato soup

1 bottle dry red wine

1 17-ounce package refrigerated cooked roast beef

1 16-ounce package frozen sugar snap stir-fry vegetables

PANTRY LIST

Dried thyme

20
MINUTES

ASIAN-STYLE BEEF SOUP

START TO FINISH: *15 minutes*

- **3 14-ounce cans beef broth**
- **1 16-ounce package loose-pack frozen broccoli stir-fry vegetables**
- **3 tablespoons teriyaki sauce**
- **2 teaspoons grated fresh ginger or ½ teaspoon ground ginger**
- **1 9-ounce package frozen cooked seasoned beef strips, thawed and cut up, or 2 cups chopped cooked beef**

1. In a large saucepan bring beef broth to boiling. Stir in frozen vegetables, teriyaki sauce, and ginger. Return to boiling; reduce heat. Simmer, covered, for 3 to 5 minutes or until vegetables are tender. Stir in beef strips; heat through.

Makes 4 servings

PER SERVING: 177 cal., 6 g total fat (2 g sat. fat), 41 mg chol., 1,885 mg sodium, 10 g carbo., 2 g fiber, 21 g pro.

SHOPPING LIST

3 14-ounce cans beef broth

1 16-ounce package loose-pack frozen broccoli stir-fry vegetables

1 8-ounce jar teriyaki sauce

1 piece fresh ginger

1 9-ounce package frozen cooked seasoned beef strips

20
MINUTES

HORSERADISH BEEF WRAPS

START TO FINISH: *10 minutes*

- **⅓ cup mayonnaise**
- **1 tablespoon prepared horseradish**
- **4 9- to 10-inch flour tortillas**
- **8 ounces sliced cooked roast beef**
- **4 slices Swiss cheese**
- **⅔ cup shredded lettuce**
- **¼ cup shredded radishes**

1. In a small bowl stir together mayonnaise and horseradish. Spread mixture on one side of each tortilla. Top with beef, cheese, lettuce, and radishes. Tightly roll up each tortilla. Serve wraps at once or, if desired, wrap in plastic wrap and refrigerate for up to 4 hours.

Makes 4 servings

PER SERVING: 455 cal., 28 g total fat (9 g sat. fat), 59 mg chol., 967 mg sodium, 25 g carbo., 1 g fiber, 22 g pro.

SHOPPING LIST

1 8-ounce jar prepared horseradish
1 package 9- to 10-inch flour tortillas
8 ounces thinly sliced cooked roast beef
1 6-ounce package sliced Swiss cheese
1 package shredded lettuce
1 bunch radishes

PANTRY LIST

Mayonnaise

20
MINUTES

CIABATTA WITH MEATBALLS AND GREENS

START TO FINISH: *15 minutes*

- **⅓ cup olive oil**
- **¼ cup lemon juice**
- **1 bunch Italian (flat-leaf) parsley, large stems removed**
- **2 cloves garlic**
- **Salt and ground black pepper**
- **1 16- to 18-ounce package frozen cooked Italian-style meatballs, thawed**
- **6 ciabatta rolls, split and toasted**
- **½ of a small head romaine lettuce, cut up or torn**

1. In a food processor or blender combine oil, lemon juice, parsley, and garlic; cover and process until finely chopped. Add salt and pepper to taste.

2. Transfer parsley mixture to a large skillet; add meatballs and cook, covered, over medium heat until heated through, stirring and spooning sauce over meatballs occasionally.

3. Place 1 ciabatta roll, toasted side up, on each of 6 plates. Top with shredded romaine. Remove meatballs from skillet with a slotted spoon; place on romaine. Drizzle with parsley mixture. Top with remaining roll halves.

Makes 6 servings

PER SERVING: 534 cal., 31 g total fat (10 g sat. fat), 49 mg chol., 1,002 mg sodium, 43 g carbo., 6 g fiber, 20 g pro.

SHOPPING LIST

1 lemon
1 bunch Italian (flat-leaf) parsley
1 16-ounce package frozen cooked Italian-style meatballs
1 head romaine lettuce
6 ciabatta rolls

PANTRY LIST

Olive oil
Garlic
Salt
Ground black pepper

20 MINUTES

MONSTER MEATBALL SUB

START TO FINISH: *20 minutes*

- **1 16-ounce package barbecue sauce with seasoned meatballs**
- **1 loaf French bread**
- **4 ounces sliced provolone cheese**
- **⅓ cup thinly sliced red onion**
- **1 small tomato, chopped**

1. Preheat broiler. Heat meatballs according to package directions.

2. Cut bread in half horizontally, cutting to but not through 1 side. Hollow out insides of bread halves, leaving 1-inch shells; set excess bread aside for another use. Place loaf, cut sides up, on a baking sheet. Top bottom side of loaf with cheese slices.

3. Broil 4 to 5 inches from the heat for 2 to 3 minutes or until cheese melts and bread is lightly toasted.

4. With a slotted spoon, remove meatballs from sauce and place on bottom half of the loaf. Sprinkle with red onion and tomato. Close loaf and cut in slices to serve. If desired, serve with remaining barbecue sauce.

Makes 6 servings

PER SERVING: 450 cal., 15 g total fat (7 g sat. fat), 32 mg chol., 1,122 mg sodium, 60 g carbo., 2 g fiber, 22 g pro.

SHOPPING LIST

1 16-ounce package barbecue sauce with seasoned meatballs

1 loaf French bread

1 6-ounce package sliced provolone cheese

1 red onion

1 small tomato

20
MINUTES

SPICY REUBEN MELTS

START TO FINISH: *20 minutes*

- **8 slices rye bread, toasted**
- **8 ounces sliced corned beef or pastrami**
- **½ cup sauerkraut, rinsed and drained**
- **12 bottled pepperoncini salad peppers, sliced**
- **4 slices Swiss cheese**
- **¼ cup bottled Thousand Island salad dressing**

1. Preheat broiler. Place 4 bread slices on a baking sheet. Top the bread slices with corned beef, sauerkraut, pepperoncini, and cheese. Broil 4 to 5 inches from the heat for 2 minutes or until cheese melts. Spread salad dressing on remaining 4 bread slices. Place bread, dressing sides down, on top of broiled sandwiches.

Makes 4 servings

PER SERVING: 394 cal., 17 g total fat (6 g sat. fat), 55 mg chol., 2,056 mg sodium, 38 g carbo., 5 g fiber, 24 g pro.

SHOPPING LIST

1 16-ounce loaf rye bread

8 ounces thinly sliced corned beef or pastrami

1 14-ounce can sauerkraut

1 16-ounce jar pepperoncini salad peppers

1 8-ounce package sliced Swiss cheese

1 16-ounce bottle Thousand Island salad dressing

20 MINUTES

PORK MEDALLIONS WITH CRANBERRY-FIG CHUTNEY

START TO FINISH: *20 minutes*

- **½ cup fresh cranberries or ¼ cup canned whole cranberry sauce**
- **¼ cup apple juice or apple cider**
- **2 tablespoons snipped dried figs**
- **1 tablespoon packed brown sugar or granulated sugar**
- **½ teaspoon snipped fresh rosemary or ¼ teaspoon dried rosemary, crushed**
- **Salt**
- **Freshly ground black pepper**
- **6 ounces pork tenderloin**
- **2 teaspoons cooking oil**

1. For chutney, in a small heavy saucepan stir together cranberries, apple juice, figs, sugar, and rosemary. Bring to boiling; reduce heat. Simmer, uncovered, for 5 to 8 minutes or until chutney is desired consistency, stirring occasionally. Season to taste with salt and pepper; set aside.

2. Meanwhile, trim fat from pork. Cut meat into 6 pieces. Press each piece with palm of your hand to make an even thickness. In a large nonstick skillet cook pork in hot oil over medium-high heat for 2 to 3 minutes or until juices run clear (160°F), turning once. Serve pork with chutney.

Makes 2 servings

PER 2½ OUNCES PORK + ¼ CUP CHUTNEY: 227 cal., 7 g total fat (1 g sat. fat), 55 mg chol., 185 mg sodium, 23 g carbo., 3 g fiber, 18 g pro.

SHOPPING LIST

1 12-ounce package fresh cranberries
1 5-ounce can apple juice
1 9-ounce package dried figs
1 package fresh rosemary
6 ounces pork tenderloin

PANTRY LIST

Brown sugar
Salt
Black pepper
Cooking oil

20
MINUTES

BALSAMIC PORK MEDALLIONS

START TO FINISH: *15 minutes*

- **2 cups sliced fresh mushrooms**
- **2 cups small broccoli florets, chopped broccoli rabe, or chopped Broccolini**
- **2 tablespoons butter**
- **12 ounces pork tenderloin**
- **Salt and ground black pepper**
- **2 ounces prosciutto, cut into bite-size strips**
- **¼ cup balsamic vinegar**
- **1 tablespoon packed brown sugar**

1. In a large skillet cook mushrooms and broccoli in 1 tablespoon of the hot butter over medium-high heat about 3 minutes or until crisp-tender, stirring occasionally. Remove vegetables from skillet; set aside.

2. Meanwhile, trim fat from pork; cut pork into ½-inch slices. Sprinkle pork with salt and pepper. Add to skillet and cook in remaining 1 tablespoon hot butter for 4 to 6 minutes or until juices run clear (160°F), turning once.

3. Add prosciutto, vinegar, brown sugar, and vegetables to skillet; heat through.

Makes 4 servings

PER SERVING: 240 cal., 10 g total fat (5 g sat. fat), 80 mg chol., 551 mg sodium, 12 g carbo., 2 g fiber, 25 g pro.

SHOPPING LIST

1 8-ounce package sliced fresh mushrooms
1 head broccoli
12 ounces pork tenderloin
2 ounces prosciutto

PANTRY LIST

Butter
Salt
Ground black pepper
Balsamic vinegar
Brown sugar

20
MINUTES

PORK MEDALLIONS ON GREEN BEANS

START TO FINISH: *20 minutes*

- **1 1- to 1½-pound honey-mustard marinated pork tenderloin**
- **1 tablespoon butter**
- **1 9-ounce package frozen French-cut green beans, thawed**
- **1 teaspoon dried dillweed**
- **1 teaspoon lemon juice**

1. Cut tenderloin into ¼-inch slices. In an extra-large skillet cook pork in hot butter over medium heat for 4 to 6 minutes or until juices run clear (160°F), turning once. Remove meat from skillet, reserving drippings in skillet. Keep warm.

2. Add green beans and dill to drippings in skillet. Cook and stir for 3 to 4 minutes or until beans are tender. Stir in lemon juice. Transfer beans to a serving platter. Serve pork on top of green beans.

Makes 4 servings

PER SERVING: 187 cal., 8 g total fat (4 g sat. fat), 53 mg chol., 549 mg sodium, 7 g carbo., 2 g fiber, 21 g pro.

SHOPPING LIST

1 pound honey-mustard marinated pork tenderloin

1 9-ounce package frozen French-cut green beans

1 small container dried dillweed

1 lemon

PANTRY LIST

Butter

20
MINUTES

JAMAICAN-STYLE PORK

START TO FINISH: *20 minutes*

- **1 16-ounce package frozen peppers and onion stir-fry vegetables**
- **1 tablespoon cooking oil**
- **12 ounces pork strips for stir-frying**
- **2 to 3 teaspoons Jamaican jerk seasoning**
- **½ cup bottled plum sauce**
- **Soy sauce (optional)**
- **Peanuts (optional)**
- **2 cups hot cooked rice or pasta**

1. In a wok or skillet cook and stir frozen vegetables in hot oil over medium-high heat for 5 to 7 minutes or until vegetables are crisp-tender. Remove from wok.

2. Toss pork strips with jerk seasoning; add to wok. Add more oil if necessary. Cook and stir for 2 to 5 minutes or until pork is no longer pink.

3. Add plum sauce to wok; return vegetables. Gently toss to coat; heat through. If desired, season with soy sauce and sprinkle with peanuts. Serve over rice.

Makes 4 servings

PER SERVING: 357 cal., 9 g total fat (2 g sat. fat), 54 mg chol., 405 mg sodium, 45 g carbo., 2 g fiber, 22 g pro.

Test Kitchen Tip: If your supermarket doesn't sell pork strips, cut them from pork loin.

SHOPPING LIST

1 16-ounce package frozen stir-fry vegetables

12 ounces pork strips for stir-frying

1 small container Jamaican jerk seasoning

1 5.5-ounce bottle plum sauce

PANTRY LIST

Cooking oil

Rice

20
MINUTES

ASIAN PORK SOUP

START TO FINISH: *20 minutes*

- **12 ounces lean boneless pork, cut into thin bite-size strips**
- **1 tablespoon cooking oil**
- **2 cups sliced fresh mushrooms**
- **2 cloves garlic, minced**
- **3 14-ounce cans reduced-sodium chicken broth**
- **2 tablespoons dry sherry**
- **2 tablespoons reduced-sodium soy sauce**
- **2 teaspoons grated fresh ginger or ½ teaspoon ground ginger**
- **¼ teaspoon crushed red pepper**
- **2 cups thinly sliced Chinese (napa) cabbage**
- **1 green onion, thinly sliced**

1. In a large saucepan cook pork strips in hot oil for 2 to 3 minutes or until slightly pink in center. Remove from pan; set aside. Add mushrooms and garlic to saucepan; cook until tender.

2. Stir in broth, sherry, soy sauce, ginger, and crushed red pepper. Bring to boiling. Stir in pork, cabbage, and green onion; heat through.

Makes 6 servings

PER SERVING: 142 cal., 6 g total fat (2 g sat. fat), 31 mg chol., 690 mg sodium, 4 g carbo., 1 g fiber, 16 g pro.

SHOPPING LIST

12 ounces lean boneless pork

1 8-ounce package sliced fresh mushrooms

3 14-ounce cans reduced-sodium chicken broth

1 small bottle dry sherry

1 10-ounce bottle reduced-sodium soy sauce

1 piece fresh ginger

1 small head Chinese (napa) cabbage

1 bunch green onions

PANTRY LIST

Cooking oil

Garlic

Crushed red pepper

20
MINUTES

CURRY PORK STIR-FRY

START TO FINISH: *20 minutes*

- **2** **6-ounce boneless pork top loin chops, cut into thin bite-size strips**
- **1** **tablespoon cooking oil**
- **1** **medium onion, chopped (½ cup)**
- **1** **medium red sweet pepper, coarsely chopped (¾ cup)**
- **2** **teaspoons curry powder**
- **1** **teaspoon bottled minced ginger or ½ teaspoon ground ginger**
- **¼** **teaspoon salt**
- **1** **14-ounce can unsweetened coconut milk**
- **1** **tablespoon cornstarch**
- **1** **cup frozen peas**
- **¼** **cup golden raisins**
- **1** **tablespoon lime juice (optional)**
- **1** **8.8-ounce pouch cooked long grain rice**

1. In a large skillet cook pork strips in hot oil over medium-high heat for 3 to 5 minutes or until brown, stirring occasionally. Remove meat from skillet. Add onion, sweet pepper, curry powder, ginger, and salt to skillet. Cook about 5 minutes or until vegetables are crisp-tender, stirring frequently. Add additional cooking oil if necessary.

2. Meanwhile, in a medium bowl whisk together coconut milk and cornstarch. Add to vegetable mixture in skillet. Cook and stir until thick and bubbly. Cook and stir for 2 minutes more. Stir in pork, peas, raisins, and, if desired, lime juice. Heat through.

3. Meanwhile, prepare rice according to package directions. Serve pork mixture over rice.

Makes 4 servings

PER SERVING: 520 cal., 28 g total fat (19 g sat. fat), 47 mg chol., 253 mg sodium, 41 g carbo., 4 g fiber, 25 g pro.

SHOPPING LIST

2 6-ounce boneless pork top loin chops
1 medium onion
1 medium red sweet pepper
1 small container curry powder
1 4-ounce bottle minced fresh ginger
1 14-ounce can unsweetened coconut milk
1 10-ounce package frozen peas
1 15-ounce package golden raisins
1 8.8-pouch cooked long grain rice

PANTRY LIST

Cooking oil
Salt
Cornstarch

20
MINUTES

PORK CHOPS WITH PEAR-MAPLE SAUCE

START TO FINISH: *20 minutes*

- **4 boneless pork loin chops, cut ¾ inch thick (about 1 pound)**
- **½ teaspoon salt**
- **½ teaspoon ground black pepper**
- **1 tablespoon olive oil**
- **¼ cup butter**
- **3 tablespoons pure maple syrup or maple-flavor syrup**
- **3 tablespoons peach, apricot, or plum preserves or jam**
- **½ teaspoon dried basil, crushed**
- **3 medium pears, cored and thinly sliced**

1. Trim fat from chops. Sprinkle chops with salt and pepper. In a large skillet cook chops in hot oil over medium-high heat for 8 to 12 minutes or until juices run clear (160°F), turning once. Remove chops from skillet; cover to keep warm.

2. For sauce, in same skillet melt butter over medium heat. Stir in maple syrup, peach preserves, and basil. Add pears. Cook, covered, about 3 minutes or just until the pears are tender and heated through, occasionally spooning sauce over pears. Serve chops with pears and sauce.

Makes 4 servings

PER SERVING: 495 cal., 23 g total fat (11 g sat. fat), 108 mg chol., 437 mg sodium, 40 g carbo., 4 g fiber, 32 g pro.

SHOPPING LIST

4 boneless pork loin chops
1 8-ounce bottle pure maple syrup
1 8- or 10-ounce jar peach preserves
3 medium pears

PANTRY LIST

Salt
Ground black pepper
Olive oil
Butter
Dried basil

20
MINUTES

PORK WITH CRANBERRIES AND SWEET POTATOES

START TO FINISH: *20 minutes*

- **4 boneless pork loin chops, cut ¾ inch thick (about 1 pound)**
- **Salt and ground black pepper**
- **Nonstick cooking spray**
- **1 17-ounce can vacuum-packed sweet potatoes**
- **1 tablespoon butter**
- **1 cup orange juice**
- **¼ cup dried cranberries**

1. Trim fat from chops. Sprinkle chops lightly with salt and pepper. Lightly coat an unheated large skillet with cooking spray. Heat skillet over medium-high heat. Add chops; cook for 8 to 12 minutes or until juices run clear (160°F), turning once. Transfer chops to a serving platter; cover to keep warm.

2. Meanwhile, place sweet potatoes in a medium saucepan. Mash with a potato masher. Stir in butter. Cook and stir over medium heat until potatoes are heated through. If desired, season with additional salt and pepper.

3. Add orange juice and cranberries to skillet. Bring to boiling; reduce heat. Simmer, uncovered, about 7 minutes or until liquid is reduced by half. Spoon sauce over chops. Serve with sweet potatoes.

Makes 4 servings

PER SERVING: 341 cal., 8 g total fat (4 g sat. fat), 78 mg chol., 226 mg sodium, 38 g carbo., 3 g fiber, 27 g pro.

SHOPPING LIST

4 boneless pork loin chops
1 17-ounce can vacuum-packed sweet potatoes
1 3-ounce package dried cranberries

PANTRY LIST

Salt
Ground black pepper
Nonstick cooking spray
Butter
Orange juice

20
MINUTES

SMOKED PORK CHOPS WITH SPICED CREAM

START TO FINISH: *15 minutes*

- **6 cooked smoked boneless pork loin chops**
- **1 teaspoon ground coriander**
- **½ teaspoon ground ginger**
- **½ teaspoon ground cinnamon**
- **¼ teaspoon ground cumin**
- **¼ teaspoon cayenne pepper**
- **Dash ground mace**
- **1 tablespoon butter**
- **¼ cup whipping cream**
- **1 tablespoon dairy sour cream**

1. Trim fat from chops. In a small bowl combine coriander, ginger, cinnamon, cumin, cayenne pepper, and mace. Remove ¼ teaspoon of the spice mixture; set aside. Rub remaining spice mixture on both sides of chops.

2. In a very large skillet cook chops in hot butter over medium heat for 8 to 10 minutes or until hot, turning once.

3. Meanwhile, in a small mixing bowl beat whipping cream with a rotary beater or wire whisk until soft peaks form (tips curl). Fold in sour cream and the reserved ¼ teaspoon spice mixture.

4. Serve chops with whipped cream mixture.

Makes 6 servings

PER SERVING: 193 cal., 12 g total fat (6 g sat. fat), 80 mg chol., 1,313 mg sodium, 1 g carbo., 0 g fiber, 20 g pro.

SHOPPING LIST

6 cooked smoked boneless pork loin chops
1 small container ground coriander
1 small container ground ginger
1 small container mace
1 8-ounce carton whipping cream
1 8-ounce carton dairy sour cream

PANTRY LIST

Ground cinnamon
Ground cumin
Cayenne pepper
Butter

20
MINUTES

TILAPIA WITH ALMOND BROWNED BUTTER

START TO FINISH: *20 minutes*

- **3 cups snow peas, trimmed**
- **4 4- to 5-ounce fresh skinless tilapia or other firm white fish fillets**
- **Salt and freshly ground black pepper**
- **1 teaspoon all-purpose flour**
- **1 tablespoon olive oil**
- **2 tablespoons butter**
- **¼ cup coarsely chopped almonds**
- **1 tablespoon snipped fresh parsley**

1. In a large saucepan bring lightly salted water to boiling. Add snow peas. Cook for 2 minutes. Drain and set aside.

2. Meanwhile, rinse fish; pat dry with paper towels. Season fish on 1 side with salt and pepper; sprinkle with flour. Measure thickness of fish. In a large skillet cook fish, flour sides up, in hot oil over medium-high heat for 4 to 6 minutes per ½-inch thickness of fish or until fish flakes when tested with a fork, turning once halfway through cooking. (If necessary, cook fish half at a time.) Arrange peas on a serving platter; place fish on top of peas.

3. Reduce heat to medium. Add butter to skillet. When butter begins to melt, stir in almonds. Cook for 30 to 60 seconds or until butter melts and nuts are lightly toasted (do not let butter burn). Spoon butter mixture over fish fillets. Sprinkle with parsley.

Makes 4 servings

PER SERVING: 266 cal., 15 g total fat (5 g sat. fat), 71 mg chol., 210 mg sodium, 7 g carbo., 3 g fiber, 24 g pro.

SHOPPING LIST

6 ounces fresh snow pea pods
4 4-ounce skinless fresh tilapia fillets
1 2-ounce package almonds
1 bunch fresh parsley

PANTRY LIST

Salt
Black pepper
All-purpose flour
Olive oil
Butter

20
MINUTES

CAJUN CATFISH AND RICE

START TO FINISH: *20 minutes*

4 6-ounce fresh catfish fillets, about ½ inch thick

3 to 4 teaspoons blackened seasoning

⅔ cup fine dry bread crumbs

3 tablespoons olive oil

1 medium onion, chopped (½ cup)

1 medium red or yellow sweet pepper, chopped (¾ cup)

2 cloves garlic, minced

1 8.8-ounce pouch cooked roasted chicken-flavor rice

1. Rinse fish; pat dry with paper towels. Sprinkle fish with 2 to 3 teaspoons of the blackened seasoning. Place bread crumbs in a shallow dish. Coat both sides of fish with bread crumbs.

2. In a very large skillet cook fish fillets in 2 tablespoons of the hot oil over medium-low to medium heat about 6 to 8 minutes or until golden brown and fish flakes when tested with a fork, carefully turning once. Remove from skillet and keep warm.

3. Add onion, sweet pepper, garlic, and the remaining 1 tablespoon oil to skillet. Cook and stir until vegetables are tender. Meanwhile, prepare rice according to package directions. Stir rice and the remaining 1 teaspoon blackened seasoning into vegetable mixture; heat through. Serve fish with rice.

Makes 4 servings

PER SERVING: 506 cal., 6 g total fat (5 g sat. fat), 80 mg chol., 904 mg sodium, 36 g carbo., 2 g fiber, 32 g pro.

SHOPPING LIST

4 6-ounce fresh catfish fillets

1 3-ounce jar blackened seasoning

1 8-ounce container fine dry bread crumbs

1 medium onion

1 medium red or yellow sweet pepper

1 8.8-ounce pouch cooked roasted chicken-flavor rice

PANTRY LIST

Olive oil

Garlic

20
MINUTES

WASABI-GLAZED SALMON WITH EDAMAME RICE SALAD

START TO FINISH: *20 minutes*

- **4 5- to 6-ounce fresh skinless salmon fillets**
- **2 tablespoons sesame ginger liquid meat marinade**
- **½ teaspoon wasabi powder**
- **1 cup frozen sweet soybeans (edamame)**
- **1 8.8-ounce pouch cooked long grain rice**
- **2 tablespoons rice vinegar**
- **2 tablespoons salad oil**
- **1 teaspoon honey**
- **1 teaspoon soy sauce**
- **½ teaspoon ground ginger**
- **⅓ cup bias-sliced green onions**

1. Preheat broiler. Rinse fish; pat dry with paper towels. Measure thickness of fish.

2. Place fish fillets on the greased unheated rack of a broiler pan, tucking under any thin edges. Broil 4 inches from the heat for 4 to 6 minutes per ½-inch thickness of fish or until fish flakes when tested with a fork. (If fillets are 1 inch or more thick, carefully turn once halfway through broiling.) In a small bowl combine sesame ginger marinade and wasabi powder. Brush on salmon the last 2 minutes of broiling.

3. Meanwhile, cook edamame according to package directions; set aside. Prepare rice according to package directions; set aside. In a screwtop jar combine rice vinegar, salad oil, honey, soy sauce, and ginger. Cover and shake well.

4. In a medium bowl combine edamame, rice, green onions, and dressing. Toss to combine. Serve with salmon.

Makes 4 servings

PER SERVING: 482 cal., 25 g total fat (4 g sat. fat), 84 mg chol., 467 mg sodium, 28 g carbo., 2 g fiber, 33 g pro.

SHOPPING LIST

4 5- to 6-ounce fresh skinless salmon fillets

1 12-ounce bottle sesame ginger liquid meat marinade

1 small container wasabi powder

1 12-ounce package frozen sweet soybeans (edamame)

1 8.8-ounce pouch cooked long grain rice

1 10-ounce bottle rice vinegar

1 small container ground ginger

1 bunch green onions

PANTRY LIST

Salad oil

Honey

Soy sauce

20
MINUTES

SALMON WITH RED CABBAGE

START TO FINISH: *20 minutes*

- **4 5-ounce fresh or frozen skinless salmon fillets**
- **¼ cup balsamic vinegar**
- **⅛ teaspoon salt**
- **¼ teaspoon ground black pepper**
- **¼ cup purchased basil pesto**
- **6 cups coarsely shredded red cabbage**
- **2 green onions, bias-sliced**

1. Thaw salmon, if frozen. Rinse fish; pat dry with paper towels. Place salmon fillets on the greased unheated rack of a broiler pan. Measure thickness of fish. Brush salmon with 1 tablespoon of the balsamic vinegar; sprinkle with salt and pepper. Broil 4 to 5 inches from heat for 4 to 6 minutes per ½-inch thickness or until salmon flakes when tested with a fork.

2. Meanwhile, in a bowl whisk together remaining vinegar and pesto until combined. Remove 2 tablespoons of the pesto mixture. Add cabbage to pesto mixture in bowl; toss to coat.

3. To serve, place cabbage mixture on plate; top with salmon. Drizzle with reserved pesto mixture. Sprinkle with green onion slices.

Makes 4 servings

PER SERVING: 329 cal., 16 g total fat (3 g sat. fat), 83 mg chol., 354 mg sodium, 14 g carbo., 3 g fiber, 31 g pro.

SHOPPING LIST

4 5-ounce fresh or frozen skinless salmon fillets

1 8-ounce container basil pesto

1 head red cabbage

1 bunch green onions

PANTRY LIST

Balsamic vinegar

Salt

Ground black pepper

20
MINUTES

CURRIED TUNA ON BISCUITS

START TO FINISH: *20 minutes*

- **3 tablespoons butter**
- **3 tablespoons all-purpose flour**
- **2 to 3 teaspoons curry powder**
- **¼ teaspoon salt**
- **2 cups milk**
- **1 12-ounce can chunk white tuna, drained**
- **1 cup frozen peas**
- **½ cup purchased coarsely shredded fresh carrot**
- **4 frozen baked biscuits for microwave**

1. In a large saucepan melt butter over medium heat. Stir in flour, curry powder, and salt. Cook and stir for 30 seconds. Add milk all at once. Cook and stir until thick and bubbly; cook and stir 1 minute more. Stir in tuna, peas, and carrot; cook and stir until heated through.

2. Meanwhile, heat biscuits according to package directions. Serve tuna mixture over split biscuits.

Makes 4 servings

PER SERVING: 494 cal., 23 g total fat (10 g sat. fat), 68 mg chol., 1,208 mg sodium, 39 g carbo., 3 g fiber, 31 g pro.

SHOPPING LIST

1 small container curry powder

1 12-ounce can chunk white tuna

1 9- to 10-ounce package frozen peas

1 16-ounce package coarsely shredded fresh carrot

1 16-ounce package freezer-to-microwave baked biscuits

PANTRY LIST

Butter

All-purpose flour

Salt

Milk

20
MINUTES

MEXICAN TUNA MELT

START TO FINISH: *20 minutes*

- **2 6-ounce cans chunk white tuna, drained**
- **¼ cup mayonnaise or salad dressing**
- **2 tablespoons toasted pumpkin seeds (pepitas)* or dry-roasted sunflower seeds**
- **½ teaspoon finely shredded lime peel**
- **1 tablespoon lime juice**
- **1 tablespoon finely chopped red onion**
- **1 teaspoon finely chopped chipotle peppers in adobo sauce (optional)****
- **8 slices whole wheat bread**
- **4 ounces Monterey Jack cheese with jalapeño peppers, shredded**
- **1 small tomato, thinly sliced**
- **1 cup packaged shredded lettuce**

1. Preheat broiler. In a medium bowl combine tuna, mayonnaise, pumpkin seeds, lime peel, lime juice, onion, and, if desired, chipotle. Place 4 of the bread slices on a baking sheet. Spread the tuna mixture on the bread slices. Top with cheese. Broil 4 to 5 inches from the heat for 1½ to 3 minutes or until cheese melts. Top with tomato slices, lettuce, and the remaining bread slices.

Makes 4 servings

PER SERVING: 467 cal., 26 g total fat (9 g sat. fat), 73 mg chol., 883 mg sodium, 24 g carbo., 4 g fiber, 36 g pro.

*Note: To toast pumpkin seeds, spread seeds in a shallow baking pan; bake in a 350°F oven for 7 to 10 minutes or until toasted. Cool.

**Note: Because hot peppers, such as chipotles, contain volatile oils that can burn your skin and eyes, avoid direct contact with chiles as much as possible. When working with chile peppers, wear plastic or rubber gloves. If your bare hands do touch chile peppers, wash your hands well with soap and water.

SHOPPING LIST

2 6-ounce cans chunk white tuna
1 6-ounce package pumpkin seeds (pepitas)
1 lime
1 red onion
1 7-ounce can chipotle peppers in adobo sauce
1 loaf whole wheat bread
1 8-ounce piece Monterey Jack cheese with jalapeño peppers
1 small tomato
1 10-ounce package shredded iceberg lettuce

PANTRY LIST

Mayonnaise

20 MINUTES

SEAFOOD OMELET WITH AVOCADO SALSA

START TO FINISH: *20 minutes*

- **1 medium avocado, halved, seeded, peeled, and chopped**
- **1 tablespoon finely chopped red onion**
- **1 tablespoon snipped fresh cilantro**
- **1 tablespoon lime juice**
- **Salt and ground black pepper**
- **8 eggs**
- **½ cup water**
- **¼ cup chopped green onions (2)**
- **¼ teaspoon salt**
- **¼ teaspoon ground black pepper**
- **¼ teaspoon cayenne pepper**
- **4 tablespoons butter**
- **1 6-ounce can crabmeat, drained, flaked, and cartilage removed, or one 7-ounce package frozen peeled, cooked tiny shrimp, thawed and patted dry**

1. For salsa, in a medium bowl combine avocado, red onion, cilantro, lime juice, and salt and pepper to taste.

2. In a large bowl combine eggs, water, green onion, ¼ teaspoon salt, ¼ teaspoon black pepper, and cayenne. Beat until combined. Heat a medium nonstick skillet over medium-high heat.

3. Add 1 tablespoon of the butter to skillet. When butter melts, add ½ cup of the egg mixture; lower heat to medium. Using a spatula, stir egg mixture gently but continuously until mixture resembles small pieces of cooked egg surrounded by liquid egg. Stop stirring. Cook 30 to 60 seconds more or until egg mixture is set but shiny.

4. Spoon one-fourth of the crab across center of eggs. With a spatula lift and fold edge of omelet about one-third of the way toward the center. Remove from heat. Fold opposite edge toward center; transfer to a warm plate. Repeat with remaining butter, egg, and filling. Serve with salsa.

Makes 4 servings

PER SERVING: 373 cal., 29 g total fat (10 g sat. fat), 493 mg chol., 665 mg sodium, 6 g carbo., 3 g fiber, 22 g pro.

SHOPPING LIST

1 medium avocado
1 small red onion
1 bunch fresh cilantro
1 8-ounce bottle lime juice
1 bunch green onions
1 small container cayenne pepper
1 6-ounce can crabmeat

PANTRY LIST

Salt
Ground black pepper
Eggs
Butter

20
MINUTES

SPICY THAI PEANUT NOODLES

START TO FINISH: *20 minutes*

- 1 **9-ounce package refrigerated linguine**
- 1 **cup packaged fresh julienne or shredded carrots**
- 1 **medium red or yellow sweet pepper, seeded and cut into thin strips**
- ½ **of a medium cucumber, seeded and cut into thin strips**
- ⅓ **cup bias-sliced green onions**
- ⅓ **cup torn fresh basil**
- 1 **11.5-ounce bottle peanut sauce**
- ⅓ **cup dry-roasted peanuts**

1. Cook linguine according to package directions; drain. Rinse under cold running water until chilled; drain again. If desired, snip pasta with clean kitchen scissors to make shorter lengths.

2. In a large bowl toss together drained pasta, carrots, sweet pepper, cucumber, green onions, and basil. Add peanut sauce and toss to coat. Sprinkle with peanuts.

Makes 4 servings

PER SERVING: 496 cal., 20 g total fat (4 g sat. fat), 68 mg chol., 1,288 mg sodium, 62 g carbo., 4 g fiber, 16 g pro.

SHOPPING LIST

1 9-ounce package refrigerated linguine

1 10-ounce package fresh julienne carrot

1 medium red sweet pepper

1 medium cucumber

1 bunch green onions

1 bunch fresh basil

1 11.5-ounce bottle peanut sauce

1 8-ounce jar dry roasted peanuts

20
MINUTES

VEGETABLE FRIED RICE

START TO FINISH: *20 minutes*

- **1 teaspoon toasted sesame oil or cooking oil**
- **2 eggs, lightly beaten**
- **⅓ cup rice vinegar**
- **¼ cup soy sauce**
- **⅛ teaspoon ground ginger**
- **⅛ teaspoon crushed red pepper**
- **1 cup sliced fresh mushrooms**
- **1 teaspoon bottled minced garlic**
- **1 tablespoon cooking oil**
- **2 8.8-ounce pouches cooked long grain rice**
- **½ cup loose-pack frozen peas**
- **1 2-ounce jar diced pimientos, drained**
- **¼ cup chopped peanuts (optional)**

1. In a large skillet heat sesame oil over medium heat. Add half of the beaten eggs, lifting and tilting the skillet to form a thin layer (egg may not completely cover the bottom of the skillet). Cook about 1 minute or until set. Invert skillet over a baking sheet to remove cooked egg; cut into strips and set aside. Repeat with remaining egg.

2. In a small bowl stir together vinegar, soy sauce, ginger, and crushed red pepper; set aside.

3. In the same skillet cook mushrooms and garlic in hot oil over medium-high heat about 3 minutes or until mushrooms are tender. Stir in vinegar mixture. Stir in rice, peas, and pimientos. Cook and stir about 2 minutes or until heated through and liquid is nearly evaporated. Stir in egg strips. If desired, sprinkle servings with chopped peanuts.

Makes 4 servings

PER SERVING: 314 cal., 10 g total fat (1 g sat. fat), 106 mg chol., 999 mg sodium, 45 g carbo., 3 g fiber, 10 g pro.

SHOPPING LIST

1 8-ounce bottle toasted sesame oil
1 10-ounce bottle rice vinegar
1 5-ounce bottle soy sauce
1 small container ground ginger
1 8-ounce package sliced fresh mushrooms
2 8.8-ounce pouches cooked long grain rice
1 10-ounce package frozen peas
1 2-ounce jar diced pimientos

PANTRY LIST

Eggs
Crushed red pepper
Cooking oil
Bottled minced garlic

20
MINUTES

POLENTA AND BLACK BEANS

START TO FINISH: *20 minutes*

- **3 cups water**
- **1 cup yellow cornmeal**
- **1 cup water**
- **½ teaspoon salt**
- **1 15-ounce can black beans, rinsed and drained**
- **1 14.5-ounce can diced tomatoes, undrained**
- **1 cup bottled salsa with cilantro or other salsa**
- **¾ cup shredded Mexican cheese blend (3 ounces)**

1. For polenta, in a large saucepan bring the 3 cups water to boiling. In a medium bowl combine cornmeal, the 1 cup water, and salt. Stir cornmeal mixture slowly into the boiling water. Cook and stir until mixture comes to boiling. Reduce heat to low. Cook for 5 to 10 minutes or until mixture is thick, stirring occasionally. (If mixture is too thick, stir in additional water.)

2. Meanwhile, in a large skillet combine beans, undrained tomatoes, and salsa. Bring mixture to boiling; reduce heat. Simmer, uncovered, for 10 minutes, stirring frequently. Stir ½ cup of the cheese into the polenta. Divide polenta among 4 shallow bowls. Top with the bean mixture and sprinkle with the remaining cheese.

Makes 4 servings

PER SERVING: 311 cal., 8 g total fat (4 g sat. fat), 19 mg chol., 751 mg sodium, 49 g carbo., 8 g fiber, 15 g pro.

SHOPPING LIST

1 24-ounce package yellow cornmeal
1 15-ounce can black beans
1 14.5-ounce can diced tomatoes
1 8-ounce jar salsa
1 8-ounce package shredded Mexican cheese blend

PANTRY LIST

Salt

TURKEY POT PIES, page 90

MEALS

30
MINUTES

MEDITERRANEAN PIZZA SKILLET

START TO FINISH: *30 minutes*

- **3 skinless, boneless chicken breast halves, cut into ¾-inch pieces**
- **2 cloves garlic, minced**
- **2 tablespoons olive oil**
- **4 roma tomatoes, chopped**
- **1 14-ounce can artichoke hearts, drained and quartered**
- **1 2.25-ounce can sliced pitted ripe olives, drained**
- **½ teaspoon dried Italian seasoning, crushed**
- **¼ teaspoon freshly ground black pepper**
- **2 cups romaine lettuce or hearty mesclun, chopped**
- **1 cup crumbled feta cheese (4 ounces)**
- **⅓ cup fresh basil leaves, shredded or torn**
- **Crusty Italian or French bread, sliced**

1. In a large skillet cook and stir chicken and garlic in hot oil over medium-high heat until chicken is brown. Stir in tomatoes, artichokes, olives, seasoning, and pepper. Bring to boiling; reduce heat. Simmer, covered, for 10 minutes or until chicken is no longer pink (170°F). Top with lettuce and cheese. Cook, covered, for 1 to 2 minutes more or until lettuce starts to wilt. Sprinkle with basil. Serve on or with bread.

Makes 4 servings

PER SERVING: 395 cal., 17 g total fat (6 g sat. fat), 82 mg chol., 1,003 mg sodium, 27 g carbo., 6 g fiber, 33 g pro.

SHOPPING LIST

3 skinless, boneless chicken breast halves
4 roma tomatoes
1 14-ounce can artichoke hearts
1 2.25-ounce can sliced pitted ripe olives
1 head romaine lettuce
1 4-ounce package feta cheese
1 small package fresh basil leaves
1 loaf Italian bread

PANTRY LIST

Garlic
Olive oil
Dried Italian seasoning
Black pepper

30
MINUTES

CARAMELIZED ONION AND CHERRY CHICKEN

START TO FINISH: *30 minutes*

- **4 skinless, boneless chicken breast halves**
- **Salt and ground black pepper**
- **2 tablespoons cooking oil**
- **1 large onion, thinly sliced**
- **¼ cup water**
- **2 tablespoons packed brown sugar**
- **2 tablespoons dried sweet cherries**
- **1 14.8-ounce pouch cooked long grain white rice**
- **Sliced green onions**

1. Season the chicken with salt and pepper. In a large skillet cook chicken in hot oil for 4 minutes, turning once. Add onion to skillet. Cook and stir for 4 minutes more or until onion is tender, turning the chicken to brown evenly. Stir in the water, brown sugar, and cherries. Cook and stir for 4 minutes or until cherries are plump, cooking liquid is slightly thick, and chicken is no longer pink (170°F).

2. Meanwhile, prepare rice according to package directions. Serve chicken and onion mixture with rice. Sprinkle with sliced green onions.

Makes 4 servings

PER SERVING: 446 cal., 11 g total fat (1 g sat. fat), 82 mg chol., 243 mg sodium, 47 g carbo., 2 g fiber, 36 g pro.

SHOPPING LIST

4 boneless, skinless chicken breast halves

1 large onion

1 3-ounce package sweetened dried cherries

1 14.8-ounce pouch cooked long grain white rice

1 bunch green onions

PANTRY LIST

Salt

Ground black pepper

Cooking oil

Brown sugar

30 MINUTES

PANFRIED CHICKEN BREASTS WITH ORANGE SAUCE

START TO FINISH: *30 minutes*

- **4 skinless, boneless chicken breast halves**
- **4 tablespoons butter**
- **½ teaspoon finely shredded orange peel**
- **3 tablespoons orange juice**
- **2 tablespoons golden raisins or raisins**
- **2 teaspoons packed brown sugar**
- **Hot cooked rice or pasta**

1. In a large skillet cook chicken in 1 tablespoon of the butter over medium-high heat for 12 minutes or until chicken is no longer pink (170°F), turning once. (Reduce heat if necessary to keep chicken from overbrowning.) Transfer chicken to a serving platter; cover and keep warm.

2. Add remaining butter to the skillet. Stir in orange peel, orange juice, raisins, and brown sugar. Cook and stir over medium heat about 2 minutes or until slightly thick. Add chicken to skillet to heat through. Serve with hot cooked rice or pasta.

Makes 4 servings

PER SERVING: 391 cal., 14 g total fat (8 g sat. fat), 113 mg chol., 478 mg sodium, 30 g carbo., 1 g fiber, 35 g pro.

SHOPPING LIST

4 skinless, boneless chicken breast halves
1 orange
1 11-ounce package golden raisins
Rice or pasta

PANTRY LIST

Butter
Brown sugar

30 MINUTES

MAPLE CHICKEN FETTUCCINE

START TO FINISH: *30 minutes*

- **10 ounces dried fettuccine**
- **5 skinless, boneless chicken breast halves**
- **Salt and ground black pepper**
- **1 tablespoon olive oil**
- **1 16-ounce package frozen sweet pepper and onion stir-fry vegetables**
- **¾ cup chicken broth**
- **1 tablespoon cornstarch**
- **1 teaspoon snipped fresh rosemary**
- **⅛ teaspoon ground black pepper**
- **¼ cup maple syrup**

SHOPPING LIST

1 12-ounce package dried fettuccine

5 skinless, boneless chicken breast halves

1 16-ounce package frozen sweet pepper and onion stir-fry vegetables

1 14-ounce can chicken broth

1 package fresh rosemary

1 8-ounce bottle maple syrup

PANTRY LIST

Salt

Ground black pepper

Olive oil

Cornstarch

1. Cook pasta according to package directions. Drain; set aside and keep warm.

2. Meanwhile, season chicken with salt and black pepper. In a very large skillet cook chicken in hot oil over medium heat for 10 to 12 minutes or until no longer pink (170°F), turning once. Remove chicken from skillet; keep warm.

3. Increase heat to medium-high. Add vegetable blend to skillet; cook and stir for 6 to 8 minutes or until vegetables are crisp-tender.

4. In a small bowl stir together broth, cornstarch, rosemary, and ⅛ teaspoon black pepper. Add to skillet. Cook and stir until thick and bubbly. Cook and stir 1 minute more. Stir in maple syrup.

5. Arrange hot pasta on 5 dinner plates or shallow bowls. Top with chicken. Spoon peppers and sauce over chicken.

Makes 5 servings

PER SERVING: 466 cal., 6 g total fat (1 g sat. fat), 79 mg chol., 285 mg sodium, 60 g carbo., 2 g fiber, 40 g pro.

30
MINUTES

LEMON CHICKEN STIR-FRY

START TO FINISH: *25 minutes*

- **1 pound skinless, boneless chicken breast halves**
- **¾ cup chicken broth**
- **3 tablespoons lemon juice**
- **1 tablespoon cornstarch**
- **1 tablespoon soy sauce**
- **1 16-ounce package frozen stir-fry vegetables (any blend)**
- **2 tablespoons cooking oil**
- **2 cups hot cooked rice**

1. Cut chicken into bite-size strips; set aside. For sauce, in a small bowl stir together broth, lemon juice, cornstarch, and soy sauce; set aside.

2. In a large skillet cook frozen vegetables in 1 tablespoon hot oil over medium-high heat for 5 to 7 minutes or until crisp-tender. Remove from skillet. Add remaining 1 tablespoon oil and half of the chicken to the skillet. Cook and stir for 2 to 3 minutes or until chicken is no longer pink (170°F). Remove from skillet. Repeat with remaining chicken (add more oil if necessary). Return all chicken to skillet. Push chicken from center of skillet.

3. Stir sauce; add to center of skillet. Cook and stir until thick and bubbly. Return vegetables to skillet; stir to coat with sauce. Cook and stir for 1 to 2 minutes more or until heated through. Serve with rice. If desired, pass additional soy sauce.

Makes 4 servings

PER SERVING: 348 cal., 9 g total fat (2 g sat. fat), 66 mg chol., 522 mg sodium, 32 g carbo., 3 g fiber, 32 g pro.

SHOPPING LIST

1 pound skinless, boneless chicken breast halves
1 14-ounce can chicken broth
1 lemon
1 5-ounce bottle soy sauce
1 16-ounce package frozen stir-fry vegetables
1 16-ounce package rice

PANTRY LIST

Cornstarch
Cooking oil

30 MINUTES

PANFRIED ITALIAN CHICKEN PARMESAN

START TO FINISH: *25 minutes*

- **8 ounces dried linguine or fettuccine**
- **1 egg**
- **1 tablespoon cooking oil**
- **½ teaspoon salt**
- **¼ teaspoon coarsely ground black pepper**
- **½ cup panko (Japanese-style bread crumbs)**
- **¼ cup grated Parmesan cheese**
- **1 teaspoon dried Italian seasoning, crushed**
- **4 skinless, boneless chicken breast halves**
- **Salt and ground black pepper**
- **2 tablespoons cooking oil**
- **1 cup prepared marinara sauce**
- **Grated Parmesan cheese**

1. Prepare pasta according to package directions; drain.

2. Meanwhile, in a shallow dish whisk together egg, 1 tablespoon oil, salt, and pepper; set aside. In another shallow dish combine panko, ¼ cup Parmesan cheese, and Italian seasoning. Sprinkle chicken lightly with salt and pepper. Dip each chicken breast half in the egg mixture and then in the bread crumb mixture to coat.

3. In large skillet cook chicken in 2 tablespoons hot oil over medium-high heat for 8 to 12 minutes or until no longer pink (170°F), turning once. (If chicken browns too quickly, reduce heat to medium.)

4. Meanwhile, place marinara sauce in microwave-safe dish. Heat on high for 1 minute or until hot. Spoon about ¼ cup sauce on each chicken breast. If desired, sprinkle with additional Parmesan cheese. Serve with hot cooked pasta.

Makes 4 servings

PER SERVING: 456 cal., 17 g total fat (4 g sat. fat), 175 mg chol., 807 mg sodium, 31 g carbo., 1 g fiber, 42 g pro.

SHOPPING LIST

1 16-ounce package dried linguine
1 8-ounce package panko (Japanese-style bread crumbs)
1 4-ounce package grated Parmesan cheese
4 skinless, boneless chicken breast halves
1 14-ounce jar marinara sauce

PANTRY LIST

Egg
Cooking oil
Salt
Ground black pepper
Dried Italian seasoning

30
MINUTES

CHICKEN WITH CREAMY MUSHROOMS

START TO FINISH: *30 minutes*

- **1 pound sliced fresh mushrooms, such as button or shiitake**
- **3 tablespoons butter**
- **6 Italian-marinated skinless, boneless chicken breast halves**
- **3 tablespoons rice vinegar or white wine vinegar**
- **1½ cups whipping cream**
- **3 tablespoons capers, drained**
- **¼ teaspoon freshly ground black pepper**

1. In an extra large skillet cook mushrooms in 1 tablespoon hot butter over medium-high heat about 5 minutes or until tender. Remove mushrooms from skillet.

2. Reduce heat to medium. Add remaining 2 tablespoons butter and chicken breast halves to skillet. Cook for 8 to 12 minutes or until no longer pink (170° F), turning once. Remove chicken from skillet and keep warm.

3. Remove skillet from heat; add vinegar, stirring to loosen browned bits on bottom of skillet. Return skillet to heat. Stir in cream, capers, and pepper. Bring to boiling; boil gently, uncovered, for 2 to 3 minutes or until sauce is slightly thick. Return mushrooms to skillet; heat through. Serve chicken with sauce.

Makes 6 servings

PER SERVING: 456 cal., 34 g total fat (19 g sat. fat), 183 mg chol., 967 mg sodium, 7 g carbo., 1 g fiber, 33 g pro.

SHOPPING LIST

2 8-ounce containers sliced fresh mushrooms

6 Italian-marinated skinless, boneless chicken breast halves

1 10-ounce bottle rice vinegar

1 8-ounce carton whipping cream

1 3.5-ounce jar capers

PANTRY LIST

Butter

Black pepper

30
MINUTES

TROPICAL BROILED CHICKEN

START TO FINISH: *30 minutes*

- **4 skinless, boneless chicken breast halves**
- **Salt and ground black pepper**
- **⅓ cup pineapple jam**
- **2 tablespoons orange juice or water**
- **1 tablespoon cooking oil**
- **1 tablespoon snipped fresh cilantro**
- **¼ teaspoon salt**
- **¼ teaspoon ground black pepper**
- **½ of a peeled, cored fresh pineapple, cut into 4 rings**

1. Preheat broiler. Place chicken breast halves on the unheated rack of a broiler pan. Sprinkle lightly with salt and pepper. Broil about 5 inches from the heat for 5 minutes. Meanwhile, in a small bowl combine jam, orange juice, oil, cilantro, ¼ teaspoon salt, and ¼ teaspoon pepper; brush over chicken. Turn chicken; add pineapple rings to pan. Broil 4 to 7 minutes more or until chicken is no longer pink (170°F), brushing chicken and pineapple with glaze the last 3 to 4 minutes of broiling. Spoon any remaining glaze over chicken breasts and serve.

Makes 4 servings

PER SERVING: 262 cal., 5 g total fat (1 g sat. fat), 66 mg chol., 374 mg sodium, 27 g carbo., 1 g fiber, 27 g pro.

SHOPPING LIST

4 skinless, boneless chicken breast halves

1 12-ounce jar pineapple jam

1 bunch cilantro

1 peeled, cored fresh pineapple

PANTRY LIST

Salt

Ground black pepper

Orange juice

Cooking oil

30
MINUTES

ITALIAN CHICKEN ORZO SOUP

START TO FINISH: *25 minutes*

2 14-ounce cans reduced-sodium chicken broth
1 pound skinless, boneless chicken breast halves or thighs, cubed
1 14.5-ounce can diced tomatoes with basil, garlic, and oregano, undrained
½ cup dried orzo
1 cup chopped zucchini
1 teaspoon finely shredded lemon peel
1 tablespoon lemon juice
Ground black pepper
4 to 6 tablespoons purchased basil pesto

1. In a large saucepan combine broth, chicken, undrained tomatoes, and orzo. Bring to boiling; reduce heat. Simmer, uncovered, for 6 minutes.

2. Add zucchini, lemon peel, and lemon juice. Return to boiling; reduce heat. Simmer, uncovered, for 3 to 4 minutes or until orzo and zucchini are tender and chicken is no longer pink (170°F). Season to taste with pepper. Ladle into bowls. Top with pesto.

Makes 4 to 6 servings

PER SERVING: 371 cal., 12 g total fat (0 g sat. fat), 68 mg chol., 1,180 mg sodium, 30 g carbo., 1 g fiber, 35 g pro.

SHOPPING LIST

2 14-ounce cans reduced-sodium chicken broth
1 pound skinless, boneless chicken breast halves
1 14.5-ounce can diced tomatoes with basil, garlic, and oregano
1 small package dried orzo
1 small zucchini
1 lemon
1 8-ounce container purchased basil pesto

PANTRY LIST

Ground black pepper

30 MINUTES

CHICKEN WITH PRETZELS AND COUSCOUS

START TO FINISH: *25 minutes*

- **1 cup pretzel sticks**
- **⅔ cup unsalted peanuts**
- **¼ to ½ teaspoon crushed red pepper**
- **½ cup refrigerated or frozen egg product, thawed**
- **14 to 16 ounces chicken breast tenderloins**
- **½ cup reduced-sodium chicken broth**
- **1 16-ounce package frozen sweet peppers and onion stir-fry vegetables**
- **½ cup uncooked couscous**
- **2 tablespoons seasoned rice vinegar**
- **1 tablespoon cooking oil**
- **Honey-Mustard Dipping Sauce**

1. Preheat oven to 425°F. Line a 15×10×1-inch pan with foil; coat with nonstick cooking spray; set pan aside. In a food processor place pretzels,½ cup of the peanuts, and crushed red pepper. Process until coarsely ground; transfer to resealable plastic bag.

2. Place egg product in shallow dish. Dip chicken into egg product; allow excess egg product to drip off. Transfer tenderloins, half at a time, to bag with crumb mixture. Seal bag; turn to coat chicken pieces. Arrange chicken in prepared pan. Bake for 10 to 15 minutes or until no longer pink (170°F).

3. Meanwhile, in a saucepan combine broth and stir-fry vegetables. Bring to boiling. Stir in couscous; remove from heat. Cover; let stand for 5 minutes. Chop remaining peanuts. Stir peanuts, rice vinegar, and oil into couscous. Serve couscous with chicken and dipping sauce.

Makes 6 servings

PER SERVING: 336 cal., 12 g total fat (2 g sat. fat), 39 mg chol., 344 mg sodium, 31 g carbo., 4 g fiber, 26 g pro.

HONEY-MUSTARD DIPPING SAUCE: In a bowl combine ⅓ cup plain yogurt, 2 tablespoons yellow mustard, and 2 teaspoons honey.

SHOPPING LIST

1 small bag pretzel sticks
1 2.25-ounce package unsalted peanuts
1 16-ounce carton refrigerated egg product
14 to 16 ounces chicken breast tenderloins
1 14-ounce can reduced-sodium chicken broth
1 16-ounce package frozen sweet pepper and onion stir-fry vegetables
1 12-ounce package couscous
1 10-ounce bottle seasoned rice vinegar
1 6-ounce carton plain yogurt

PANTRY LIST

Crushed red pepper
Cooking oil
Yellow mustard
Honey

30 MINUTES

CHICKEN-HOMINY CHILI

START TO FINISH: *30 minutes*

- **1 pound skinless, boneless chicken breast halves, cut into 1-inch pieces**
- **1 tablespoon cooking oil**
- **2 14-ounce cans reduced-sodium chicken broth**
- **2 15- to 16-ounce cans navy beans, rinsed and drained**
- **1 15.5-ounce can white hominy, rinsed and drained**
- **1 4-ounce can diced green chile peppers**
- **1 teaspoon ground cumin**
- **¼ teaspoon ground black pepper**
- **4 ounces Monterey Jack cheese with jalapeño peppers, shredded**

1. In a Dutch oven cook chicken, half at a time, in hot oil over medium heat until no longer pink (170°F). Return all chicken to the Dutch oven.

2. Stir in broth, navy beans, hominy, green chiles, cumin, and pepper. Bring to boiling; reduce heat. Simmer, covered, for 15 minutes.

3. Using a potato masher, gently mash the mixture to crush about half of the beans. Stir in cheese; heat just until cheese melts.

Makes 4 to 6 servings

PER SERVING: 601 cal., 15 g total fat (7 g sat. fat), 91 mg chol., 1,962 mg sodium, 62 g carbo., 14 g fiber, 53 g pro.

SHOPPING LIST

1 pound skinless, boneless chicken breast halves

2 14-ounce cans reduced-sodium chicken broth

2 15-ounce cans navy beans

1 15.5-ounce can white hominy

1 4-ounce can diced green chile peppers

1 8-ounce package shredded Monterey Jack cheese with jalapeño peppers

PANTRY LIST

Cooking oil

Ground cumin

Ground black pepper

30
MINUTES

RASPBERRY-DIJON CHICKEN SALAD

START TO FINISH: *30 minutes*

- **¼ cup seedless raspberry preserves**
- **1 tablespoon Dijon-style mustard**
- **1 tablespoon bottled balsamic vinaigrette salad dressing**
- **4 skinless, boneless chicken breast halves**
- **¼ teaspoon salt**
- **⅛ teaspoon ground black pepper**
- **8 cups torn mixed salad greens**
- **1 cup cherry tomatoes, halved**
- **¼ cup chopped pecans, toasted**
- **⅓ cup bottled balsamic vinaigrette salad dressing**

1. Preheat broiler. In a small bowl stir together preserves, mustard, and 1 tablespoon dressing; set aside. Season chicken with salt and pepper; place on the unheated rack of a broiler pan. Broil 4 to 5 inches from the heat for 3 minutes per side. Brush 1 side with preserves mixture. Broil 2 minutes more. Turn and brush with remaining mixture. Broil 2 minutes more or until no longer pink (170°F). Remove from oven; cover with foil and set aside.

2. In a very large bowl toss together greens, tomatoes, pecans, and ⅓ cup dressing. Divide among 4 serving plates. Slice chicken and place on greens.

Makes 4 servings

PER SERVING: 355 cal., 14 g total fat (2 g sat. fat), 82 mg chol., 606 mg sodium, 22 g carbo., 3 g fiber, 35 g pro.

SHOPPING LIST

1 12-ounce jar seedless raspberry preserves
1 16-ounce bottle balsamic vinaigrette salad dressing
4 skinless, boneless chicken breast halves
1 8-ounce package torn mixed salad greens
1 pint cherry tomatoes
1 4-ounce package chopped pecans

PANTRY LIST

Dijon-style mustard
Salt
Ground black pepper

30 MINUTES

LICKETY-SPLIT LEMON CHICKEN

START TO FINISH: *30 minutes*

- **12 ounces chicken breast tenderloins**
- **2 tablespoons butter**
- **1 8-ounce package sliced mushrooms**
- **1 medium red sweet pepper, cut into strips**
- **2 tablespoons all-purpose flour**
- **1 14-ounce can chicken broth**
- **1 teaspoon finely shredded lemon peel**
- **2 tablespoons lemon juice**
- **1 teaspoon dried thyme, crushed**
- **Salt and ground black pepper**
- **1 14.8-ounce pouch cooked long grain white rice**
- **Lemon wedges (optional)**

1. In a very large skillet cook chicken in hot butter over medium heat for 6 to 8 minutes or until no longer pink (170°F). Add mushrooms and red pepper for the last 5 minutes of cooking time. Stir in flour. Cook and stir for 1 minute more. Add chicken broth, lemon peel, lemon juice, and thyme. Cook and stir until thick and bubbly. Cook and stir for 2 minutes more. Season to taste with salt and black pepper.

2. Meanwhile, prepare rice according to package directions. Serve chicken mixture over rice. If desired, serve with lemon wedges.

Makes 4 servings

PER SERVING: 361 cal., 10 g total fat (4 g sat. fat), 66 mg chol., 643 mg sodium, 41 g carbo., 2 g fiber, 25 g pro.

SHOPPING LIST

12 ounces chicken breast tenderloins
1 8-ounce package sliced mushrooms
1 medium red sweet pepper
1 14-ounce can chicken broth
1 lemon
1 small container dried thyme
1 14.8-ounce pouch cooked long grain white rice

PANTRY LIST

Butter
All-purpose flour
Salt
Ground black pepper

30 MINUTES

COCONUT CHICKEN WITH PINEAPPLE-MANGO SALSA

START TO FINISH: *30 minutes*

- **1 egg, lightly beaten**
- **1 tablespoon cooking oil**
- **¼ teaspoon salt**
- **⅛ teaspoon cayenne pepper**
- **1¼ cups flaked coconut**
- **14 to 16 ounces chicken breast tenderloins**
- **1 8-ounce can pineapple tidbits (juice pack), drained**
- **1 cup chopped refrigerated mango slices (about 10 slices)**
- **2 tablespoons snipped fresh cilantro (optional)**
- **1 tablespoon lime juice**
- **¼ teaspoon salt**

1. Preheat oven to 400°F. Line a large baking sheet with foil; lightly grease foil. Set aside. In a shallow dish whisk together egg, oil, salt, and cayenne pepper. Spread coconut in another shallow dish. Dip chicken, 1 piece at a time, in egg mixture, allowing excess to drip off. Coat chicken in coconut and arrange on prepared baking sheet. Bake for 10 to 12 minutes or until chicken is no longer pink (170°F).

2. Meanwhile, for salsa, in a medium bowl combine pineapple, mango, cilantro (if using), lime juice, and salt. Serve with chicken.

Makes 4 servings

PER SERVING: 401 cal., 18 g total fat (12 g sat. fat), 110 mg chol., 485 mg sodium, 33 g carbo., 3 g fiber, 27 g pro.

SHOPPING LIST

1 8-ounce package flaked coconut

14 to 16 ounces chicken breast tenderloins

1 8-ounce can pineapple tidbits

1 20-ounce jar refrigerated mango slices

1 lime

PANTRY LIST

Egg

Cooking oil

Salt

Cayenne pepper

30
MINUTES

ARROZ CON POLLO

START TO FINISH: *25 minutes*

- **1 purchased roasted chicken**
- **1 14.5-ounce can diced tomatoes**
- **1 4-ounce can diced green chiles**
- **1 cup frozen peas**
- **⅓ cup pitted green olives, sliced**
- **1 8.8-ounce pouch cooked Spanish-style rice**
- **⅓ cup shredded Monterey Jack cheese**

1. Remove chicken meat from bones, discarding skin and bones. Tear chicken into large pieces. Set aside 3 cups of the chicken; save remaining chicken for another use.

2. In a large skillet combine undrained tomatoes, undrained diced green chiles, peas, and olives. Bring to boiling. Stir in rice and 3 cups chicken; heat through. Top each serving with cheese.

Makes 4 servings

PER SERVING: 399 cal., 14 g total fat (4 g sat. fat), 102 mg chol., 939 mg sodium, 29 g carbo., 4 g fiber, 37 g pro.

SHOPPING LIST

1 purchased roasted chicken
1 14.5-ounce can diced tomatoes
1 4-ounce can diced green chiles
1 9-ounce package frozen peas
1 6-ounce can pitted green olives
1 8.8-ounce pouch cooked Spanish-style rice
1 8-ounce package shredded Monterey Jack cheese

30 MINUTES

PERUVIAN-STYLE CHICKEN TACOS

START TO FINISH: *30 minutes*

- **1 pound uncooked ground chicken**
- **½ cup chopped onion (1 medium)**
- **2 teaspoons ground coriander**
- **2 teaspoons ground cumin**
- **1 teaspoon salt**
- **1 14.5-ounce can diced tomatoes, undrained**
- **1 potato, peeled and finely chopped**
- **¼ cup snipped pitted dried plums**
- **¼ cup chopped pimiento-stuffed green olives**
- **12 6- to 7-inch corn or flour tortillas**
- **4 to 6 ounces Cotija or Monterey Jack cheese, shredded**
- **Chopped onion (optional)**
- **Snipped fresh cilantro (optional)**

1. Preheat oven to 350°F. In a large skillet cook chicken and onion until chicken is no longer pink (170°F), stirring to break up pieces. Drain off fat if necessary. Add coriander, cumin, and salt; cook and stir for 1 to 2 minutes. Add undrained tomatoes, potato, plums, and olives. Bring to boiling; reduce heat. Simmer, covered, for 12 to 15 minutes or until potato is tender. Uncover; cook 5 minutes more or until most of the liquid has evaporated.

2. Wrap tortillas in foil; bake for 15 minutes or until heated. To assemble, place ⅓ cup chicken mixture in center of each tortilla; top with cheese. If desired, sprinkle with chopped onion and snipped cilantro. Fold tortillas in half.

Makes 4 servings (3 tacos each)

PER TACO: 194 cal., 10 g total fat (0 g sat. fat), 9 mg chol., 328 mg sodium, 18 g carbo., 3 g fiber, 11 g pro.

SHOPPING LIST

1 pound uncooked ground chicken
1 medium onion
1 small container ground coriander
1 14.5-ounce can diced tomatoes
1 medium potato
1 9-ounce package pitted dried plums
1 5-ounce jar pimiento-stuffed green olives
12 6-inch tortillas
4 ounces Cotija cheese

PANTRY LIST

Ground cumin
Salt

30
MINUTES

TURKEY POT PIES

START TO FINISH: *30 minutes*

- ½ **of a 15-ounce package rolled refrigerated unbaked piecrust (1 crust)**
- 1 **2.75-ounce envelope country gravy mix**
- 2 **6-ounce packages refrigerated cooked turkey breast strips**
- 1 **10-ounce package frozen mixed vegetables**
- 1 **cup milk**
- 2 **teaspoons onion powder**

1. Preheat oven to 425°F. Let piecrust stand at room temperature while preparing filling. In a medium saucepan prepare gravy mix according to package directions. Stir in turkey, vegetables, milk, and onion powder. Cook and stir until heated through. Spoon mixture into six 10-ounce ramekins or individual baking dishes; set aside.

2. Meanwhile, unroll piecrust. Using a pizza cutter, cut piecrust into 12 wedges. Place 2 wedges over turkey mixture in each ramekin. Place ramekins in a shallow baking pan. Bake for 15 minutes or until crust is golden.

Makes 6 servings

PER SERVING: 333 cal., 14 g total fat (6 g sat. fat), 33 mg chol., 975 mg sodium, 34 g carbo., 3 g fiber, 17 g pro.

SHOPPING LIST

1 15-ounce package refrigerated piecrusts

1 2.75-ounce package country gravy mix

2 6-ounce packages refrigerated cooked turkey breast strips

1 10-ounce package frozen mixed vegetables

1 small container onion powder

PANTRY LIST

Milk

30
MINUTES

TURKEY PANINI WITH BASIL AIOLI

START TO FINISH: *30 minutes*

- **2 tablespoons mayonnaise or salad dressing**
- **1 tablespoon purchased basil pesto**
- **4 ciabatta rolls, split, or 8 slices sourdough bread**
- **8 ounces thinly sliced cooked turkey breast**
- **1 3.5-ounce package thinly sliced pepperoni**
- **½ cup bottled roasted red sweet peppers, sliced**
- **4 slices provolone cheese (about 4 ounces)**
- **1 to 2 tablespoons olive oil**

1. Preheat an electric sandwich press, covered indoor grill, grill pan, or skillet. In a small bowl combine mayonnaise and pesto. Spread pesto mixture on the cut sides of the rolls. Divide turkey, pepperoni, peppers, and cheese among roll bottoms. Add roll tops. Lightly brush tops and bottoms of sandwiches with olive oil.

2. Place sandwiches (half at a time if necessary) in the sandwich press or indoor grill; cook, covered, for 7 to 9 minutes or until bread is toasted and cheese melts. (If using a grill pan or skillet, place sandwiches on grill pan. Weight sandwiches with a heavy skillet and grill about 2 minutes or until bread is lightly toasted. Turn sandwiches over, weight, and grill about 2 minutes or until second side is lightly toasted.)

Makes 4 sandwiches

PER SERVING: 506 cal., 30 g total fat (11 g sat. fat), 80 mg chol., 1,534 mg sodium, 30 g carbo., 2 g fiber, 29 g pro.

SHOPPING LIST

1 10-ounce jar basil pesto

1 package ciabatta rolls

8 ounces thinly sliced cooked turkey breast

1 3.5-ounce package thinly sliced pepperoni

1 12-ounce jar roasted red sweet peppers

1 6-ounce package sliced provolone cheese

PANTRY LIST

Mayonnaise

Olive oil

30
MINUTES

TURKEY DINNER BURGERS

START TO FINISH: *30 minutes*

- **1 egg, lightly beaten**
- **½ teaspoon salt**
- **¼ teaspoon ground black pepper**
- **1 pound uncooked ground turkey or ground chicken**
- **¼ cup fine dry bread crumbs**
- **¼ cup jalapeño pepper jelly, melted**
- **Shredded red cabbage, thinly sliced red onion, and/or other desired toppings**
- **4 ciabatta rolls, potato rolls, kaiser rolls, or hamburger buns, split and toasted**

1. Preheat boiler. In a large bowl combine egg, salt, and pepper. Add turkey and bread crumbs; mix well. Shape mixture into four ¾-inch-thick patties.

2. Place patties on the unheated rack of a broiler pan. Broil 4 to 5 inches from the heat for 12 to 14 minutes (165°F), turning once halfway through cooking time. Brush patties with half of the jalapeño jelly. Broil 1 minute; turn and brush with remaining jelly. Broil 1 minute more.

3. To assemble, place cabbage, red onion, and/or other desired toppings on bottoms of rolls. Top with patties and roll tops.

Makes 4 servings

PER SERVING: 354 cal., 12 g total fat (3 g sat. fat), 142 mg chol., 789 mg sodium, 37 g carbo., 2 g fiber, 27 g pro.

SHOPPING LIST

1 pound uncooked ground turkey
1 8-ounce package fine dry bread crumbs
1 10-ounce jar jalapeño jelly
1 small head cabbage
1 small red onion
4 ciabatta rolls

PANTRY LIST

Egg
Salt
Ground black pepper

30
MINUTES

BEEF AND POLENTA WITH RED ONION TOPPER

START TO FINISH: *30 minutes*

- **1 large red onion, cut into thin slivers**
- **2 cloves garlic, minced**
- **2 tablespoons olive oil**
- **1 cup cherry tomatoes, halved**
- **½ teaspoon dried basil or oregano, crushed**
- **Salt and ground black pepper**
- **4 beef tenderloin steaks or 2 top loin steaks, cut ¾ inch thick (about 1 pound total)**
- **Salt and ground black pepper**
- **½ of a 16-ounce tube refrigerated cooked polenta with wild mushrooms, cut into 4 slices**
- **¼ cup finely shredded Parmesan cheese**

SHOPPING LIST

1 large red onion
1 pint cherry tomatoes
1 small container dried basil
4 beef tenderloin steaks
1 16-ounce tube refrigerated cooked polenta with wild mushrooms
1 8-ounce package finely shredded Parmesan cheese

PANTRY LIST

Olive oil
Garlic
Salt
Ground black pepper

1. In a very large skillet cook and stir onion and garlic in hot oil over medium-high heat until onion is just tender. Add cherry tomatoes and basil; cook for 2 minutes more. Use a slotted spoon to remove from skillet to a bowl. Season to taste with salt and pepper. Cover and keep warm.

2. Meanwhile, sprinkle steaks with salt and pepper. If using top loin steaks, cut in half crosswise. Add steaks and polenta slices to skillet. Reduce heat to medium; cook until steak is desired doneness, turning once halfway through cooking time. For tenderloin steaks, allow 7 to 9 minutes for medium-rare (145°F) to medium (160°F) doneness. For top loin steaks, allow 10 to 12 minutes for medium-rare to medium doneness.

3. Transfer steaks and polenta slices to 4 dinner plates. Spoon red onion mixture on top. Sprinkle with Parmesan cheese.

Makes 4 servings

PER SERVING: 403 cal., 20 g total fat (6 g sat. fat), 89 mg chol., 426 mg sodium, 14 g carbo., 2 g fiber, 39 g pro.

30 MINUTES

GREEK BEEF AND PASTA SKILLET

START TO FINISH: *30 minutes*

- **8 ounces dried rotini**
- **12 ounces boneless beef sirloin steak or top round steak**
- **1 tablespoon cooking oil**
- **1 26-ounce jar ripe olive and mushroom pasta sauce, ripe olive and green olive pasta sauce, or marinara pasta sauce**
- **¼ teaspoon salt**
- **¼ teaspoon ground cinnamon**
- **½ of a 10-ounce package frozen chopped spinach, thawed and well drained**
- **⅓ cup crumbled feta cheese**

1. Cook pasta according to package directions; drain. Meanwhile, trim fat from beef. Thinly slice meat across the grain into bite-size strips.

2. In a large skillet cook and stir meat strips in hot oil for 2 to 3 minutes or until brown. Add pasta sauce, salt, and cinnamon. Cook and stir until sauce bubbles. Add cooked pasta and spinach. Cook and stir until heated through. Sprinkle with feta cheese.

Makes 4 servings

PER SERVING: 483 cal., 12 g total fat (3 g sat. fat), 63 mg chol., 1,063 mg sodium, 60 g carbo., 6 g fiber, 32 g pro.

SHOPPING LIST

1 16-ounce package dried rotini

12 ounces boneless beef sirloin steak

1 26-ounce jar ripe olive and mushroom pasta sauce

1 10-ounce package frozen chopped spinach

1 4-ounce container feta cheese

PANTRY LIST

Cooking oil

Salt

Ground cinnamon

30
MINUTES

STEAKS WITH TOMATO SALSA

START TO FINISH: *25 minutes*

- **½ teaspoon salt**
- **½ teaspoon ground cumin**
- **½ teaspoon chili powder**
- **½ teaspoon dried oregano, crushed**
- **½ teaspoon packed brown sugar**
- **2 8-ounce boneless beef ribeye steaks, cut ½ to ¾ inch thick**
- **½ cup chopped onion (1 medium)**
- **2 cloves garlic, minced**
- **2 tablespoons olive oil**
- **2 cups red and/or yellow cherry or pear tomatoes, halved**
- **1 canned chipotle pepper in adobo sauce, drained and finely chopped***
- **2 tablespoons lime juice**
- **¼ cup snipped fresh cilantro**

1. In a bowl stir together ¼ teaspoon salt, cumin, chili powder, oregano, and brown sugar. Rub into both sides of steaks. Lightly coat a grill pan with nonstick cooking spray. Heat pan over medium-high heat. Add steaks. Reduce heat to medium. Cook for 8 to 10 minutes or until desired doneness (145°F for medium-rare or 160°F for medium), turning occasionally.

2. For salsa, in large skillet cook and stir onion and garlic in hot oil over medium heat until tender. Stir in tomatoes, chipotle, lime juice, and remaining ¼ teaspoon salt. Cook and stir for 1 minute. Transfer to a bowl; stir in cilantro. Cut each steak in half; serve with salsa.

Makes 4 servings

PER SERVING: 267 cal., 14 g total fat (4 g sat. fat), 54 mg chol., 451 mg sodium, 8 g carbo., 2 g fiber, 26 g pro.

*Note: Because hot chile peppers, such as chipotles, contain volatile oils that can burn your skin and eyes, avoid direct contact with chiles as much as possible. When working with chile peppers, wear plastic or rubber gloves. If your bare hands do touch the chile peppers, wash your hands well with soap and water.

SHOPPING LIST

1 16-ounce package brown sugar
2 8-ounce boneless beef ribeye steaks
1 medium onion
1 pint cherry tomatoes
1 7-ounce can chipotle peppers in adobo sauce
1 lime
1 bunch fresh cilantro

PANTRY LIST

Salt
Ground cumin
Chili powder
Dried oregano
Garlic
Olive oil

30
MINUTES

BEEF-VEGETABLE PASTA TOSS

START TO FINISH: *25 minutes*

- **1 9-ounce package refrigerated fettuccine or linguine**
- **12 ounces boneless beef sirloin steak**
- **1 teaspoon dried Italian seasoning, crushed**
- **1 tablespoon olive oil**
- **1 medium onion, cut into thin wedges**
- **2 teaspoons bottled minced garlic (4 cloves)**
- **¼ teaspoon crushed red pepper**
- **1 14.5-ounce can diced tomatoes with basil, garlic, and oregano, undrained**
- **1 cup bottled roasted red sweet peppers, drained and coarsely chopped**
- **1 tablespoon balsamic vinegar**
- **2 cups fresh baby spinach leaves**
- **¼ cup finely shredded Parmesan cheese (1 ounce)**

1. Cook pasta according to package directions. Drain well. Return pasta to hot pan. Using kitchen shears, snip pasta in a few places to break up long pieces. Cover and keep warm. Meanwhile, trim fat from beef. Sprinkle meat evenly with Italian seasoning; rub in with your fingers. Thinly slice meat across the grain.

2. In a large skillet cook and stir beef in hot oil over medium-high heat for 3 to 4 minutes or until brown; remove from skillet using a slotted spoon. Add onion, garlic, and crushed red pepper to skillet. Cook about 5 minutes or until onion is tender, stirring occasionally.

3. Stir meat, undrained tomatoes, roasted red peppers, and balsamic vinegar into onion mixture in skillet. Heat through. Add meat mixture and spinach to hot pasta; toss to mix. Sprinkle with Parmesan cheese.

Makes 4 servings

PER SERVING: 413 cal., 10 g total fat (3 g sat. fat), 123 mg chol., 687 mg sodium, 50 g carbo., 3 g fiber, 30 g pro.

SHOPPING LIST

1 9-ounce package refrigerated fettuccine

12 ounces boneless beef sirloin steak

1 medium onion

1 14.5-ounce can diced tomatoes with basil, garlic, and oregano

1 7-ounce bottle roasted red sweet peppers

1 5-ounce package fresh baby spinach leaves

1 8-ounce package finely shredded Parmesan cheese

PANTRY LIST

Dried Italian seasoning

Olive oil

Bottled minced garlic

Crushed red pepper

Balsamic vinegar

30
MINUTES

BEEF STIR-FRY SALAD

START TO FINISH: *25 minutes*

- **1 9- to 10-ounce package chopped hearts of romaine**
- **12 ounces beef top round steak (about ¾ inch thick)**
- **Salt and ground black pepper**
- **1 tablespoon cooking oil**
- **1 medium red sweet pepper, cut into strips**
- **¾ cup packaged coarsely shredded fresh carrots**
- **½ cup chopped green onions**
- **½ cup chopped dry-roasted peanuts**
- **Bottled sesame-ginger salad dressing**

1. Divide lettuce among 4 plates, set aside.

2. Thinly slice beef into bite-size strips. Season meat with salt and pepper. In a large skillet cook meat strips in hot oil over medium-high heat for 4 to 5 minutes or until brown. Add red pepper and carrots; cook and stir for 1 minute more. Remove skillet from heat; stir in green onions.

3. Spoon meat mixture over romaine on each plate. Sprinkle with peanuts. Drizzle with dressing. Serve immediately.

Makes 4 servings

PER SERVING: 393 cal., 25 g total fat (4 g sat. fat), 47 mg chol., 520 mg sodium, 17 g carbo., 4 g fiber, 25 g pro.

SHOPPING LIST

1 9- to 10-ounce package chopped hearts of romaine

12 ounces beef top round steak

1 medium sweet red pepper

1 10-ounce package coarsely shredded fresh carrots

1 bunch green onions

1 8-ounce jar dry-roasted peanuts

1 16-ounce bottle sesame-ginger dressing

PANTRY LIST

Salt

Ground black pepper

Cooking oil

30
MINUTES

SPEEDY BEEF STIR-FRY

START TO FINISH: *30 minutes*

- **1 8.8-ounce pouch cooked long grain rice**
- **1 pound boneless beef top loin steak, trimmed of fat and cut into thin strips**
- **2 tablespoons cooking oil**
- **1 16-ounce package frozen broccoli stir-fry vegetable blend**
- **½ cup orange juice**
- **1 tablespoon soy sauce**
- **2 teaspoons cornstarch**
- **1 teaspoon ground ginger**
- **¼ teaspoon crushed red pepper**
- **¼ teaspoon salt**
- **Toasted sliced almonds (optional)**

1. Heat rice according to package directions; set aside.

2. In a large skillet cook beef strips in 1 tablespoon hot oil over medium-high heat until brown; remove from skillet. Add stir-fry vegetables and the remaining 1 tablespoon oil to skillet. Cook until tender. Drain any excess liquid.

3. In a small bowl combine orange juice, soy sauce, cornstarch, ginger, crushed red pepper, and salt.

4. Return meat to skillet. Add sauce mixture to skillet; cook and stir until thick and bubbly. Serve over rice. If desired, sprinkle with toasted almonds.

Makes 4 servings

PER SERVING: 377 cal., 14 g total fat (3 g sat. fat), 60 mg chol., 500 mg sodium, 31 g carbo., 3 g fiber, 31 g pro.

SHOPPING LIST

1 8.8-ounce pouch cooked long grain rice

1 pound boneless beef top loin steak

1 16-ounce package frozen broccoli stir-fry vegetables

1 5-ounce bottle soy sauce

1 small container crushed red pepper

PANTRY LIST

Cooking oil

Orange juice

Cornstarch

Ground ginger

Salt

30
MINUTES

SOUTHWESTERN STROGANOFF

START TO FINISH: *25 minutes*

- **1 pound ground beef**
- **1 small onion, cut into thin wedges**
- **1 10-ounce can diced tomatoes and green chiles, undrained**
- **1 15- to 16-ounce can pinto beans, rinsed and drained**
- **½ cup dairy sour cream Southwestern ranch or Mexican-style dip**
- **1 tablespoon all-purpose flour**
- **4 purchased corn muffins,* split**

1. In a large skillet cook ground beef and onion until meat is brown and onion is tender; drain fat. Stir in tomatoes and green chiles and pinto beans. Heat through.

2. In a small bowl whisk together dip and flour until smooth; add to mixture in skillet. Cook and stir until thickened and bubbly. Cook and stir 1 minute more. Spoon mixture over split corn muffins.

Makes 4 servings

PER SERVING: 640 cal., 35 g total fat (13 g sat. fat), 115 mg chol., 1,072 mg sodium, 50 g carbo., 7 g fiber, 32 g pro.

*Note: If you can't find corn muffins at your bakery, lightly coat four 3-inch muffin cups with nonstick cooking spray. Prepare one 8.5-ounce package corn muffin mix according to package directions. Divide batter among prepared cups. Bake in a 400°F oven for 12 minutes or until golden.

SHOPPING LIST

1 pound ground beef

1 small onion

1 10-ounce can diced tomatoes and green chiles

1 15-ounce can pinto beans

1 8-ounce container dairy sour cream Southwestern-style dip

4 corn muffins

PANTRY LIST

All-purpose flour

30
MINUTES

STOVETOP LASAGNA

START TO FINISH: *30 minutes*

- **1 pound lean ground beef**
- **1 large onion, chopped (1 cup)**
- **1 clove garlic, minced**
- **3 cups dried mini lasagna noodles or dried extra-wide noodles**
- **1 24- to 26-ounce jar tomato and basil pasta sauce**
- **1 cup water**
- **1 cup low-fat cottage cheese or ricotta cheese**
- **1 cup shredded Italian cheese blend or mozzarella cheese**
- **¼ cup grated Parmesan cheese**
- **1 tablespoon snipped fresh parsley (optional)**

1. In very large skillet cook and stir ground beef, onion, and garlic over medium-high heat until meat is brown and onion is tender. Stir in noodles, pasta sauce, and the water. Bring to boiling; reduce heat. Cook, covered, for 15 minutes or until noodles are tender and liquid is absorbed.

2. Meanwhile, combine cottage cheese, Italian cheese blend, Parmesan cheese, and, if desired, parsley. Drop by spoonfuls over meat mixture. Simmer, covered, for 5 minutes more or until cheese melts.

Makes 6 servings

PER SERVING: 532 cal., 19 g total fat (8 g sat. fat), 69 mg chol., 736 mg sodium, 54 g carbo., 4 g fiber, 34 g pro.

SHOPPING LIST

1 pound lean ground beef
1 medium onion
1 16-ounce package dried mini lasagna noodles
1 24- to 26-ounce jar tomato and basil pasta sauce
1 15-ounce carton low-fat cottage cheese
1 8-ounce package shredded Italian cheese blend
1 8-ounce container grated Parmesan cheese

PANTRY LIST

Garlic

30 MINUTES

PASTA WITH BEEF AND ASPARAGUS

START TO FINISH: *30 minutes*

- **8 ounces boneless beef top sirloin steak**
- **1 pound fresh asparagus**
- **8 ounces dried bow tie pasta**
- **1 8-ounce carton dairy sour cream**
- **2 tablespoons all-purpose flour**
- **⅔ cup water**
- **1 tablespoon honey**
- **½ teaspoon salt**
- **¼ teaspoon ground black pepper**
- **2 tablespoons finely chopped shallot**
- **1 teaspoon cooking oil**
- **2 teaspoons snipped fresh tarragon**

1. If desired, partially freeze beef before slicing. Cut off and discard woody bases from fresh asparagus. If desired, scrape off scales. Bias-slice asparagus into 1-inch pieces; set aside. Cook pasta according to package directions, adding asparagus for the last 3 minutes of cooking. Drain well; keep warm.

2. Meanwhile, trim fat from beef. Thinly slice meat across the grain into bite-size strips. In a medium bowl stir together sour cream and flour. Stir in the water, honey, salt, and pepper. Set aside.

3. In a large nonstick skillet cook and stir meat strips and shallot in hot oil over medium-high heat about 5 minutes or until brown. Drain off fat.

4. Stir sour cream mixture into meat mixture in skillet. Cook and stir until thick and bubbly. Cook and stir for 1 minute more. Stir in drained pasta, asparagus, and tarragon. Heat through.

Makes 4 servings

PER SERVING: 421 cal., 11 g total fat (4 g sat. fat), 107 mg chol., 373 mg sodium, 54 g carbo., 3 g fiber, 26 g pro.

SHOPPING LIST

8 ounces boneless beef top sirloin steak

1 pound fresh asparagus

1 16-ounce package dried bow tie pasta

1 8-ounce carton dairy sour cream

1 shallot

1 package fresh tarragon

PANTRY LIST

All-purpose flour

Honey

Salt

Ground black pepper

Cooking oil

30
MINUTES

MAPLE-GLAZED PORK MEDALLIONS

START TO FINISH: *30 minutes*

- **1½ cups water**
- **¾ cup uncooked long grain white rice**
- **¼ teaspoon salt**
- **1 1- to 1¼-pound pork tenderloin, cut into ¾-inch slices**
- **2 teaspoons cooking oil**
- **1 large red cooking apple, cored and cut into ½-inch wedges**
- **⅓ cup pure maple syrup**
- **2 tablespoons water**
- **¼ teaspoon salt**
- **½ teaspoon finely chopped canned chipotle peppers in adobo sauce (optional)***

SHOPPING LIST

1 16-ounce package long grain white rice

1 1- to 1¼-pound pork tenderloin

1 large red cooking apple

1 8-ounce bottle pure maple syrup

1 7-ounce can chipotle peppers in adobo sauce

PANTRY LIST

Salt

Cooking oil

1. In a large saucepan combine 1½ cups water, rice, and ¼ teaspoon salt. Bring to boiling over high heat; reduce heat to low. Cook, covered, for 15 minutes or until rice is tender and liquid is absorbed.

2. Meanwhile, in a large skillet cook pork in hot oil over medium-high heat for 6 to 8 minutes or until slightly pink (160°F). Remove meat from skillet; set aside.

3. Add apple wedges to skillet. Cook and stir for 2 minutes. Add syrup, 2 tablespoons water, ¼ teaspoon salt, and, if using, chipotle peppers. Cook and stir until boiling; boil gently for 2 to 3 minutes or until apples are just tender. Add meat to skillet; heat through. Serve meat mixture over rice.

Makes 4 servings

PER SERVING: 394 cal., 9 g total fat (2 g sat. fat), 75 mg chol., 354 mg sodium, 52 g carbo., 2 g fiber, 27 g pro.

*Note: Because hot chile peppers, such as chipotles, contain volatile oils that can burn your skin and eyes, avoid direct contact with chiles as much as possible. When working with chile peppers, wear plastic or rubber gloves. If your bare hands do touch the chile peppers, wash your hands well with soap and water.

30 MINUTES

PEACHY PORK CHILI

START TO FINISH: *30 minutes*

- **1 pound lean boneless pork**
- **1 tablespoon cooking oil**
- **2 14.5-ounce cans diced tomatoes, undrained**
- **2 15.5-ounce cans butter beans, rinsed and drained**
- **1½ cups chopped fresh or frozen peaches**
- **1 medium green sweet pepper, seeded and chopped (¾ cup)**
- **1 5.25-ounce can hot-style vegetable juice**
- **2 to 3 teaspoons finely chopped canned chipotles in adobo sauce***
- **Salt and ground black pepper**

1. Trim fat from pork. Cut meat into bite-size pieces. In a 4-quart Dutch oven brown meat, half at a time, in hot oil over medium heat.

2. Add undrained tomatoes, drained beans, peaches, sweet pepper, vegetable juice, and chipotles. Bring to boiling; reduce heat. Simmer, covered, for 15 minutes. Season to taste with salt and pepper.

Makes 6 servings

PER SERVING: 279 cal., 6 g total fat (2 g sat. fat), 48 mg chol., 1,130 mg sodium, 30 g carbo., 6 g fiber, 25 g pro.

*Note: Because hot chile peppers, such as chipotles, contain volatile oils that can burn your skin and eyes, avoid direct contact with chiles as much as possible. When working with chile peppers, wear plastic or rubber gloves. If your bare hands do touch the chile peppers, wash your hands well with soap and water.

SHOPPING LIST

1 pound lean boneless pork
2 14.5-ounce cans diced tomatoes
2 15.5-ounce cans butter beans
3 medium peaches
1 medium green sweet pepper
1 5.25-ounce can hot-style vegetable juice
1 7-ounce can chipotle peppers in adobo sauce

PANTRY LIST

Cooking oil
Salt
Ground black pepper

30
MINUTES

PORK SOFT-SHELL TACOS

START TO FINISH: *25 minutes*

- **8 ounces boneless pork loin**
- **2 teaspoons cooking oil**
- **¼ cup dairy sour cream**
- **¼ teaspoon ground chipotle chile pepper, crushed dried chipotle chile pepper, or chili powder**
- **4 6-inch flour tortillas, warmed***
- **½ cup shredded lettuce**
- **½ cup diced tomato**
- **½ cup shredded cheddar cheese (2 ounces)**
- **Bottled salsa**

1. If desired, partially freeze pork for easier slicing. Trim fat from pork. Thinly slice meat across the grain into bite-size strips. In a large skillet cook pork strips in hot oil over medium-high heat until done; set aside.

2. In a small bowl combine sour cream and chipotle chili powder; set aside.

3. Spoon one-fourth of the meat on each tortilla just below the center. Top meat with lettuce, tomato, and cheese. Fold top half of each tortilla over filling. Serve with sour cream mixture and salsa.

Makes 4 servings

PER SERVING: 307 cal., 17 g total fat (6 g sat. fat), 53 mg chol., 329 mg sodium, 17 g carbo., 1 g fiber, 20 g pro.

*Note: To warm tortillas, wrap them in foil. Place in a 350°F oven for 10 to 15 minutes or until warm.

SHOPPING LIST

8 ounces boneless pork loin
1 8-ounce carton dairy sour cream
1 small container ground chipotle pepper
1 package 6-inch flour tortillas
1 head lettuce
1 large tomato
1 8-ounce package shredded cheddar cheese
Bottled salsa

PANTRY LIST

Cooking oil

30
MINUTES

PEACH-GLAZED IOWA CHOPS

START TO FINISH: *25 minutes*

- **4 pork loin chops, cut 1 inch thick**
- **Salt and ground black pepper**
- **¾ cup peach or apricot preserves**
- **2 tablespoons lemon juice**
- **1 tablespoon cooking oil**
- **2 teaspoons Dijon-style mustard**

1. Preheat broiler. Season meat with salt and pepper. Place chops on the unheated rack of a broiler pan. Broil 5 to 6 inches from the heat for 6 minutes. Meanwhile, in a small bowl combine preserves, lemon juice, oil, and mustard; brush or spoon some over chops. Turn chops. Broil about 6 minutes more or until done (155°F), spooning glaze over chops the last 3 minutes of broiling. Spoon any remaining glaze on chops before serving.

Makes 4 servings

PER SERVING: 591 cal., 16 g total fat (5 g sat. fat), 177 mg chol., 393 mg sodium, 42 g carbo., 1 g fiber, 63 g pro.

SHOPPING LIST

4 pork loin chops, cut 1 inch thick

1 12-ounce jar peach or apricot preserves

1 lemon

PANTRY LIST

Salt

Ground black pepper

Cooking oil

Dijon-style mustard

30 MINUTES

PORK CHOPS WITH PLUM-GRAPE SAUCE

START TO FINISH: *25 minutes*

- **4 boneless pork top loin chops, cut 1 inch thick**
- **¼ teaspoon salt**
- **¼ teaspoon ground black pepper**
- **2 teaspoons olive oil**
- **⅓ cup water**
- **¼ cup plum jam**
- **1 tablespoon balsamic vinegar**
- **2 teaspoons Dijon-style mustard**
- **½ teaspoon chicken bouillon granules**
- **1 clove garlic, minced**
- **1 small plum, seeded and cut into thin wedges**
- **½ cup seedless red grapes, halved**
- **Snipped fresh chives (optional)**

1. Trim fat from chops. Sprinkle both sides of chops with salt and pepper. In a large nonstick skillet cook chops in hot oil over medium heat for 8 to 12 minutes or until juices run clear (160°F), turning once. Transfer chops to a serving platter. Cover and keep warm.

2. Add the water, jam, balsamic vinegar, mustard, chicken bouillon granules, and garlic to the skillet. Whisk over medium heat until bubbly. Remove from heat. Gently stir in plum wedges and grapes. To serve, spoon plum-grape mixture over chops. If desired, sprinkle with snipped chives.

Makes 4 servings

PER SERVING: 305 cal., 10 g total fat (3 g sat. fat), 83 mg chol., 386 mg sodium, 21 g carbo., 1 g fiber, 31 g pro.

SHOPPING LIST

4 boneless pork top loin chops
1 10-ounce jar plum jam
1 2.25-ounce jar chicken bouillon granules
1 small plum
1 small bunch seedless red grapes

PANTRY LIST

Salt
Ground black pepper
Olive oil
Balsamic vinegar
Dijon-style mustard
Garlic

30 MINUTES

SOUTHWEST PORK SALSA STEW

START TO FINISH: *25 minutes*

- **Nonstick cooking spray**
- **12 ounces boneless pork loin, trimmed of fat and cut into bite-size strips**
- **1 14-ounce can reduced-sodium chicken broth**
- **1 6-ounce can tomato paste**
- **½ cup bottled cilantro-flavor salsa or regular salsa**
- **½ teaspoon ground cumin**
- **1 medium zucchini, halved lengthwise and thinly sliced (2 cups)**
- **1 cup frozen sweet soybeans (edamame) or baby lima beans**
- **1 small mango, pitted, peeled, and chopped (about ½ cup)***

1. Lightly coat a large saucepan with nonstick cooking spray. Heat over medium-high heat. Add pork to hot pan; cook and stir for 2 minutes or until brown.

2. Add broth, tomato paste, salsa, and cumin; stir until combined. Stir in zucchini and soybeans. Bring to boiling; reduce heat. Simmer, covered, for 10 minutes or until vegetables are tender. Top with chopped mango.

Makes 4 servings

PER SERVING: 243 cal., 7 g total fat (2 g sat. fat), 47 mg chol., 810 mg sodium, 21 g carbo., 5 g fiber, 26 g pro.

*Test Kitchen Tip: Instead of fresh mango, use refrigerated mango slices, rinsed, drained, and chopped; or use frozen chopped mango, thawed.

SHOPPING LIST

12 ounces boneless pork loin
1 14-ounce can reduced-sodium chicken broth
1 6-ounce can tomato paste
1 16-ounce jar bottled cilantro-flavor salsa
1 medium zucchini
1 12-ounce package frozen sweet soybeans
1 small mango

PANTRY LIST

Nonstick cooking spray
Ground cumin

30
MINUTES

ITALIAN SAUSAGE AND POTATO SKILLET

START TO FINISH: *30 minutes*

- **1 pound bulk sweet Italian sausage**
- **1 medium onion, chopped (½ cup)**
- **1 stalk celery, chopped (½ cup)**
- **1 clove garlic, minced**
- **4 cups frozen diced hash brown potatoes, thawed**
- **2 14.5-ounce cans diced tomatoes with basil, garlic, and oregano, undrained**
- **1 10-ounce package frozen chopped spinach, thawed and drained**
- **1 cup finely shredded cheddar cheese (4 ounces)**

1. In a very large skillet cook and stir sausage, onion, celery, and garlic over medium heat until onion is tender and sausage is no longer pink. Drain fat. Stir in potatoes and undrained tomatoes; bring to boiling. Reduce heat. Simmer, covered, for 10 minutes or until potatoes are tender, stirring occasionally. Stir in spinach. Sprinkle with cheese. Cook, covered, for 2 minutes or until cheese melts.

Makes 6 servings

PER SERVING: 611 cal., 39 g total fat (15 g sat. fat), 74 mg chol., 1,382 mg sodium, 46 g carbo., 5 g fiber, 24 g pro.

SHOPPING LIST

1 pound bulk sweet Italian sausage
1 medium onion
1 bunch celery
1 16-ounce bag frozen diced hash brown potatoes
2 14.5-ounce cans diced tomatoes with basil, garlic, and oregano
1 10-ounce package frozen chopped spinach
1 8-ounce piece cheddar cheese

PANTRY LIST

Garlic

30
MINUTES

PASTA WITH HAM, DRIED TOMATOES, AND CHEESE

START TO FINISH: *30 minutes*

- **1 16-ounce package dried bow tie pasta**
- **1¼ cups half-and-half or light cream**
- **2 egg yolks**
- **½ teaspoon garlic salt**
- **6 ounces cooked ham, cut into bite-size strips**
- **1 cup shredded Italian cheese blend**
- **½ cup oil-packed dried tomatoes, well drained and chopped**
- **2 green onions, thinly sliced (¼ cup)**

1. In a 4-quart Dutch oven cook pasta according to package directions. Drain pasta and return to pan; cover to keep warm.

2. Meanwhile, in a medium saucepan whisk together half-and-half, egg yolks, and garlic salt. Cook and stir over medium heat until just bubbly. Pour sauce over hot cooked pasta. Add ham, cheese, and tomatoes. Stir to combine. Cook over medium-low heat until heated through. Stir before serving. Sprinkle each serving with green onions.

Makes 6 servings

PER SERVING: 473 cal., 15 g total fat (7 g sat. fat), 114 mg chol., 719 mg sodium, 61 g carbo., 3 g fiber, 23 g pro.

SHOPPING LIST

1 16-ounce package bow tie pasta
1 pint half-and-half
1 8-ounce cooked ham slice
1 8-ounce package shredded Italian cheese blend
1 8-ounce jar oil-packed dried tomatoes
1 bunch green onions

PANTRY LIST

Eggs
Garlic salt

30 MINUTES

SALMON WITH FETA AND PASTA

START TO FINISH: *25 minutes*

- **12 ounces fresh or frozen skinless salmon fillet**
- **8 ounces dried rotini**
- **Nonstick cooking spray**
- **2 cloves garlic, minced**
- **Salt**
- **4 large roma tomatoes, chopped (2 cups)**
- **1 cup sliced green onions (8)**
- **⅓ cup sliced pitted ripe olives**
- **3 tablespoons snipped fresh basil**
- **½ teaspoon coarsely ground black pepper**
- **2 teaspoons olive oil**
- **1 4-ounce package crumbled feta cheese**
- **Fresh basil sprigs (optional)**

1. Thaw fish, if frozen. Rinse fish; pat dry with paper towels. Cut fish into 1-inch pieces. Cook pasta according to pasta directions. Drain. Keep warm.

2. Meanwhile, lightly coat a large nonstick skillet with cooking spray. Heat skillet over medium-high heat. Add garlic; cook and stir for 15 seconds. Lightly season fish pieces with salt. Add fish to skillet. Cook fish for 4 to 6 minutes or until fish flakes when tested with a fork, turning fish pieces occasionally. Stir in tomatoes, onions, olives, basil, and pepper. Heat through.

3. In a large bowl toss together hot pasta, olive oil, salmon mixture, and cheese. If desired, garnish with basil sprigs.

Makes 5 servings

PER SERVING: 373 cal., 13 g total fat (5 g sat. fat), 56 mg chol., 443 mg sodium, 41 g carbo., 3 g fiber, 24 g pro.

SHOPPING LIST

12 ounces fresh or frozen skinless salmon fillet
1 16-ounce package dried rotini
4 large roma tomatoes
1 bunch green onions
1 2.25-ounce can sliced pitted ripe olives
1 package fresh basil
1 4-ounce package crumbled feta cheese

PANTRY LIST

Nonstick cooking spray
Garlic
Salt
Black pepper
Olive oil

30
MINUTES

ISLAND SALMON

START TO FINISH: *30 minutes*

- **6 5-ounce fresh salmon fillets**
- **½ cup pineapple juice**
- **¼ cup lemon juice**
- **1 tablespoon finely shredded lemon peel**
- **3 tablespoons packed brown sugar**
- **1 tablespoon chili powder**
- **1 teaspoon ground cumin**
- **¾ teaspoon salt**
- **¼ teaspoon ground cinnamon**

1. Preheat oven to 450°F. Rinse salmon; pat dry with paper towels. Place salmon in a large resealable plastic bag set in a shallow dish. Pour pineapple and lemon juice over salmon. Seal bag and marinate in the refrigerator for 15 minutes.

2. Meanwhile, in a small bowl combine lemon peel, brown sugar, chili powder, cumin, salt, and cinnamon; set aside.

3. Remove salmon from marinade, discarding marinade. Place salmon, skin sides down, on a greased shallow baking pan. Rub lemon peel mixture over salmon. Bake, uncovered, for 4 to 6 minutes per ½-inch thickness of fish or until fish flakes when tested with a fork.

Makes 6 servings

PER SERVING: 306 cal., 16 g total fat (3 g sat. fat), 84 mg chol., 392 mg sodium, 11 g carbo., 1 g fiber, 29 g pro.

SHOPPING LIST

6 5-ounce boneless salmon fillets
1 8-ounce can pineapple juice
1 lemon

PANTRY LIST

Brown sugar
Chili powder
Ground cumin
Salt
Ground cinnamon

30
MINUTES

NUT-CRUSTED SALMON WITH SLAW

START TO FINISH: *30 minutes*

- **4** **4- to 5-ounce fresh or frozen skinless salmon fillets**
- **Nonstick cooking spray**
- **3** **tablespoons orange marmalade**
- **½** **cup finely chopped walnuts**
- **¼** **teaspoon salt**
- **¼** **teaspoon ground black pepper**
- **3** **cups packaged shredded cabbage with carrot (coleslaw mix)**
- **⅓** **cup bottled ranch salad dressing**
- **1** **tablespoon honey mustard**

1. Thaw salmon, if frozen. Rinse salmon; pat dry with paper towels. Preheat oven to 450°F. Lightly coat a 2-quart square baking dish with nonstick cooking spray. Measure thickness of fish. Place fish in baking dish. Spread tops and sides of fish with marmalade. Sprinkle evenly with nuts, salt, and ⅛ teaspoon of the pepper.

2. Bake until fish flakes when tested with a fork (allow 4 to 6 minutes per ½-inch thickness of fish).

3. Meanwhile, in a large bowl stir together cabbage mix, dressing, honey mustard, and remaining ⅛ teaspoon pepper; toss to coat. Serve salmon with slaw.

Makes 4 servings

PER SERVING: 403 cal., 26 g total fat (3 g sat. fat), 69 mg chol., 372 mg sodium, 17 g carbo., 2 g fiber, 25 g pro.

SHOPPING LIST

4 4-ounce fresh or frozen skinless salmon fillets
1 10-ounce jar orange marmalade
1 2.25-ounce package chopped walnuts
1 16-ounce package shredded cabbage with carrot (coleslaw mix)
1 8-ounce bottle ranch salad dressing
1 6-ounce bottle honey mustard

PANTRY LIST

Nonstick cooking spray
Salt
Ground black pepper

30
MINUTES

SALAD NIÇOISE ON FLATBREAD

START TO FINISH: *25 minutes*

- **4 ounces fresh green beans, trimmed (if desired), and cut into 1-inch pieces (about 1 cup)**
- **1 12-ounce can chunk white or light tuna (water pack), drained and flaked**
- **1 cup halved cherry tomatoes**
- **⅓ cup chopped pitted niçoise or kalamata olives**
- **¼ cup finely chopped sweet onion (such as Vidalia, Walla Walla, or Maui)**
- **2 tablespoons snipped fresh mint**
- **1 tablespoon lemon juice**
- **2 teaspoons olive oil**
- **⅛ teaspoon ground black pepper**
- **3 cups packaged mesclun (mixed salad greens)**
- **3 Greek pita flatbreads**

1. In a medium saucepan cook green beans, covered, in boiling water about 4 minutes or until crisp-tender. Drain. Rinse under cold water; drain again.

2. Place green beans in a large bowl. Stir in tuna, cherry tomatoes, olives, onion, and mint. Add lemon juice, oil, and pepper; toss to combine. Stir in mesclun.

3. To serve, cut pita flatbreads in half crosswise. Split each pita half to form a pocket. Fill each pita pocket with about ½ cup of the tuna mixture.

Makes 6 servings

PER SERVING: 210 cal., 5 g total fat (1 g sat. fat), 24 mg chol., 527 mg sodium, 23 g carbo., 3 g fiber, 17 g pro.

SHOPPING LIST

4 ounces fresh green beans
1 12-ounce can chunk white tuna (water-pack)
1 pint cherry tomatoes
1 5-ounce jar niçoise olives
1 small sweet onion
1 package fresh mint
1 lemon
1 8-ounce package mesclun
1 package Greek pita flatbreads

PANTRY LIST

Olive oil
Ground black pepper

30 MINUTES

SOUTHWESTERN SHRIMP

START TO FINISH: *30 minutes*

- **1½ pounds fresh or frozen peeled and deveined medium shrimp***
- **2 cloves garlic, minced**
- **1 teaspoon ground chipotle chile pepper**
- **½ teaspoon ground cumin**
- **¼ teaspoon salt**
- **1 tablespoon cooking oil**
- **½ teaspoon finely shredded lime peel**
- **2 tablespoons lime juice**
- **1 teaspoon honey**
- **3 tablespoons snipped fresh cilantro**
- **1 14.8-ounce pouch cooked long grain white rice**
- **1 15-ounce can black beans, rinsed and drained**

1. If frozen, place shrimp in a bowl of cool water; let stand for 10 minutes. Drain well. In a large bowl combine shrimp, garlic, chile pepper, cumin, and salt. In a large skillet cook and stir shrimp mixture in hot oil over medium-high heat for 2 to 3 minutes or until shrimp are opaque. Remove from heat. Stir in lime peel, 1 tablespoon of the lime juice, honey, and 1 tablespoon of the cilantro.

2. Meanwhile, heat rice according to package directions. In a medium bowl combine rice, black beans, remaining 2 tablespoons cilantro, and remaining 1 tablespoon lime juice. Serve rice mixture with shrimp mixture.

Makes 6 servings

PER SERVING: 303 cal., 6 g total fat (1 g sat. fat), 172 mg chol., 534 mg sodium, 35 g carbo., 4 g fiber, 28 g pro.

*Note: If shrimp have intact tails, allow about 5 minutes to remove tails.

SHOPPING LIST

1½ pounds fresh or frozen peeled and deveined medium shrimp

1 small container ground chipotle chile pepper

1 lime

1 bunch fresh cilantro

1 14.8-ounce pouch cooked long grain white rice

1 15-ounce can black beans

PANTRY LIST

Garlic

Ground cumin

Salt

Cooking oil

Honey

30
MINUTES

SHRIMP PO'BOY

START TO FINISH: *30 minutes*

- **1 12-ounce package frozen medium shrimp**
- **2 teaspoons Old Bay seasoning**
- **¼ teaspoon ground black pepper**
- **1 tablespoon cooking oil**
- **1 cup purchased deli coleslaw**
- **2 teaspoons prepared horseradish**
- **½ teaspoon bottled hot pepper sauce**
- **4 French or hoagie rolls, split and toasted**
- **Potato chips or corn chips (optional)**

1. Place shrimp in a medium bowl half-filled with cool water. Let stand for 5 minutes; drain. Remove tails, if present. In the same bowl toss shrimp with Old Bay seasoning and pepper.

2. In a large skillet cook shrimp in hot oil over medium-high heat for 3 minutes or until opaque.

3. In a small mixing bowl combine coleslaw, horseradish, and hot pepper sauce. To serve, divide shrimp among roll bottoms. Top with coleslaw mixture. Add roll tops. If desired, serve with chips.

Makes 4 servings

PER SERVING: 545 cal., 14 g total fat (3 g sat. fat), 132 mg chol., 1,158 mg sodium, 77 g carbo., 4 g fiber, 29 g pro.

SHOPPING LIST

1 12-ounce package frozen medium uncooked shrimp
1 6-ounce container Old Bay seasoning
½ pint deli coleslaw
1 8-ounce jar prepared horseradish
1 package French rolls

PANTRY LIST

Ground black pepper
Cooking oil
Bottled hot pepper sauce

30 MINUTES

SHRIMP AND PEA POD STUFFED PEPPERS

START TO FINISH: *30 minutes*

- **4 small or 2 large sweet peppers**
- **1 3-ounce package shrimp- or mushroom-flavor ramen noodles**
- **8 ounces frozen peeled and deveined cooked shrimp**
- **⅓ cup bottled hoisin or stir-fry sauce**
- **1½ cups chopped bok choy**
- **¾ cup pea pods, strings and tips removed and halved, or ½ of a 6-ounce package frozen pea pods, thawed and halved**
- **4 green onions, thinly sliced**
- **¼ teaspoon crushed red pepper (optional)**
- **2 teaspoons toasted sesame seeds**

SHOPPING LIST

4 small sweet peppers

1 3-ounce package shrimp-flavor ramen noodles

8 ounces frozen peeled and deveined cooked shrimp

1 8-ounce bottle hoisin sauce

1 bunch bok choy

2 ounces fresh pea pods

1 bunch green onions

1 small container sesame seeds

1. Cut tops off small peppers or halve large peppers lengthwise. Remove membranes and seeds. In a 4-quart Dutch oven cook peppers in boiling water for 3 minutes. Remove; drain peppers, cut sides down, on paper towels.

2. For filling, break noodles. In a saucepan cook noodles and seasoning according to package directions. Add shrimp and cook for 30 seconds. Drain noodle mixture, discarding liquid. Return noodle mixture to pot. Add hoisin sauce, bok choy, pea pods, green onions, and, if desired, crushed red pepper; heat through.

3. Arrange peppers, cut sides up, on a serving platter. Spoon filling into peppers. Spoon any remaining filling around peppers. Sprinkle with toasted sesame seeds. Serve warm or refrigerate and serve cold.

Makes 4 servings

PER SERVING: 256 cal., 6 g total fat (2 g sat. fat), 111 mg chol., 1,050 mg sodium, 33 g carbo., 4 g fiber, 19 g pro.

30
MINUTES

BOW TIE PASTA WITH FRESH MOZZARELLA

START TO FINISH: *30 minutes*

- **1 16-ounce package dried bow tie pasta**
- **3 tablespoons olive oil**
- **4 large roma tomatoes, seeded and chopped, or 2 cups cherry tomatoes, halved**
- **1 15-ounce can cannellini beans (white kidney beans), rinsed and drained**
- **8 ounces fresh mozzarella cheese, cubed**
- **¼ cup finely shredded Parmesan cheese**
- **¼ cup snipped fresh basil or 1 teaspoon dried basil, crushed**
- **2 cloves garlic, minced**
- **¼ teaspoon salt**

1. In a 5- to 6-quart Dutch oven cook pasta according to package directions; drain and return to pan. Add olive oil and toss with pasta to coat. Add tomatoes, cannellini beans, mozzarella and Parmesan cheeses, basil, garlic, and salt; toss gently to coat.

Makes 6 servings

PER SERVING: 513 cal., 17 g total fat (7 g sat. fat), 29 mg chol., 385 mg sodium, 69 g carbo., 6 g fiber, 24 g pro.

SHOPPING LIST

1 16-ounce package dried bow tie pasta
4 large roma tomatoes
1 15-ounce can cannellini beans (white kidney beans)
8 ounces fresh mozzarella cheese
1 8-ounce package finely shredded Parmesan cheese
1 bunch fresh basil

PANTRY LIST

Olive oil
Garlic
Salt

30 MINUTES

CHEESE RAVIOLI WITH ROASTED PEPPER SAUCE

START TO FINISH: *25 minutes*

- **1 16-ounce package refrigerated 3-cheese ravioli or two 9-ounce packages refrigerated 4-cheese ravioli**
- **1 25- to 32-ounce jar roasted red pepper marinara sauce**
- **1 2.25-ounce can sliced pitted ripe olives, drained**
- **1 4-ounce can mushroom stems and pieces, drained**
- **½ cup finely chopped green sweet pepper**
- **¾ cup whipping cream**
- **¼ cup shredded fresh basil (optional)**

1. In a large saucepan cook ravioli according to package directions. Drain well.

2. Meanwhile, in a medium saucepan combine marinara sauce, drained olives, drained mushrooms, green pepper, and whipping cream. Heat over medium heat until bubbly, stirring frequently. If desired, stir in basil. Divide ravioli among 6 plates. Pour sauce over ravioli; serve immediately.

Makes 6 servings

PER SERVING: 467 cal., 26 g total fat (15 g sat. fat), 98 mg chol., 1,018 mg sodium, 44 g carbo., 6 g fiber, 13 g pro.

SHOPPING LIST

1 16-ounce package refrigerated 3-cheese ravioli

1 25-ounce jar roasted red pepper marinara sauce

1 2.25-ounce can sliced pitted ripe olives

1 4-ounce can mushroom stems and pieces

1 green sweet pepper

1 ½-pint carton whipping cream

1 bunch fresh basil

PEPPERCORN STEAKS, *page 153*

MEALS

40
MINUTES

GREEK-STYLE CHICKEN SKILLET

START TO FINISH: *40 minutes*

- **4 skinless, boneless chicken breast halves**
- **Salt and ground black pepper**
- **1 tablespoon olive oil or cooking oil**
- **1 medium zucchini, sliced (about 1½ cups)**
- **1 medium green sweet pepper, chopped (¾ cup)**
- **1 medium onion, sliced and separated into rings**
- **2 cloves garlic, minced**
- **⅛ teaspoon ground black pepper**
- **¼ cup water**
- **1 10.75-ounce can condensed tomato soup**
- **2 cups hot cooked couscous***
- **½ cup crumbled feta cheese (2 ounces)**
- **Lemon wedges**

1. Season chicken with salt and black pepper. In a large skillet cook chicken in hot oil over medium heat for 12 to 15 minutes or until no longer pink (170°F), turning once. Remove chicken from skillet; keep warm.

2. Add zucchini, sweet pepper, onion, garlic, and ⅛ teaspoon black pepper to skillet. Add the water; reduce heat. Cover and cook for 5 minutes, stirring once or twice. Stir in tomato soup. Bring to boiling; reduce heat. Simmer, covered, for 5 minutes, stirring once.

3. To serve, divide couscous among 4 dinner plates. Place chicken on couscous. Spoon vegetable mixture over chicken and couscous. Sprinkle with feta cheese. Serve with lemon wedges.

Makes 4 servings

PER SERVING: 401 cal., 10 g total fat (4 g sat. fat), 99 mg chol., 827 mg sodium, 36 g carbo., 4 g fiber, 41 g pro.

*Note: For 2 cups cooked couscous, in a small saucepan bring 1 cup water and dash salt to boiling. Stir in ⅔ cup quick-cooking couscous. Remove from heat. Cover and let stand for 5 minutes. Fluff with a fork before serving.

SHOPPING LIST

4 skinless, boneless chicken breast halves
1 medium zucchini
1 medium green sweet pepper
1 medium onion
1 10.75-ounce can condensed tomato soup
1 8-ounce package couscous
1 4-ounce package feta cheese
1 lemon

PANTRY LIST

Salt
Ground black pepper
Olive oil
Garlic

40
MINUTES

GARLIC CHICKEN AND NOODLES

START TO FINISH: *40 minutes*

- **4 skinless, boneless chicken breast halves**
- **¼ teaspoon salt**
- **¼ teaspoon ground black pepper**
- **1 tablespoon olive oil**
- **6 cloves garlic, thickly sliced**
- **½ cup chicken broth**
- **1 12-ounce package frozen home-style egg noodles**
- **¾ cup whipping cream**
- **2 tablespoons white wine vinegar or cider vinegar**
- **Snipped fresh parsley**

SHOPPING LIST

4 skinless, boneless chicken breast halves
1 14-ounce can chicken broth
1 12-ounce package frozen home-style egg noodles
1 8-ounce carton whipping cream
1 bottle white wine vinegar
1 bunch fresh parsley

PANTRY LIST

Salt
Ground black pepper
Olive oil
Garlic

1. Sprinkle both sides of chicken with salt and pepper. In a large skillet cook chicken in hot oil over medium-high heat for 5 minutes or until brown, turning once. Remove chicken from skillet. Add garlic to skillet; cook and stir for 30 seconds. Add broth; bring to boiling, stirring to loosen any browned bits from bottom of skillet. Return chicken to skillet. Reduce heat to medium-low; cover and cook about 15 minutes or until chicken is no longer pink (170°F).

2. Meanwhile, cook noodles according to package directions; drain.

3. Remove chicken from skillet; cover to keep warm. Increase heat to medium-high. Add cream and vinegar to skillet. Bring to boiling; boil gently about 5 minutes or until thick, stirring occasionally.

4. Serve chicken with noodles. Spoon cream sauce over chicken and noodles and top with snipped fresh parsley.

Makes 4 servings

PER SERVING: 594 cal., 25 g total fat (12 g sat. fat), 243 mg chol., 391 mg sodium, 48 g carbo., 2 g fiber, 41 g pro.

40
MINUTES

CHICKEN WITH PAN SAUCE

START TO FINISH: *35 minutes*

- **4 skinless, boneless chicken breast halves**
- **¼ teaspoon salt**
- **¼ teaspoon freshly ground black pepper**
- **5 tablespoons cold butter**
- **⅔ cup dry white wine**
- **½ cup chicken broth**
- **¼ cup finely chopped shallots or onion**
- **2 tablespoons whipping cream**

SHOPPING LIST

4 skinless, boneless chicken breast halves

1 bottle dry white wine

1 14-ounce can chicken broth

2 shallots

1 8-ounce carton whipping cream

PANTRY LIST

Salt

Black pepper

Butter

1. Place 1 chicken breast half between 2 pieces of plastic wrap. Using the flat side of a meat mallet, pound the chicken lightly to about ¼ inch thick. Remove plastic wrap. Repeat with remaining chicken. Sprinkle chicken with salt and pepper.

2. In a large skillet cook chicken in 1 tablespoon hot butter over medium heat for 6 to 8 minutes or until no longer pink (170°F), turning once. Transfer chicken to a platter; cover with foil to keep warm.

3. Add wine, broth, and shallots to hot skillet. Cook and stir to scrape up browned bits from the bottom of the pan. Bring to boiling. Boil gently for 10 to 15 minutes or until liquid is reduced to ¼ cup. Reduce heat to medium-low.

4. Stir cream into skillet. Add remaining 4 tablespoons butter, 1 tablespoon at a time, stirring after each addition until butter melts. Sauce should be slightly thick. Season to taste with additional salt and pepper. Serve sauce over chicken.

Makes 4 servings

PER BREAST HALF + 2 TABLESPOONS SAUCE: 325 cal., 20 g total fat (10 g sat. fat), 117 mg chol., 444 mg sodium, 2 g carbo., 0 g fiber, 27 g pro.

40 MINUTES

PRONTO PASTA

START TO FINISH: *40 minutes*

- **8 ounces dried fettuccine, linguine, or spaghetti**
- **2 teaspoons dried thyme, crushed**
- **1½ teaspoons lemon-pepper seasoning**
- **½ teaspoon bottled minced garlic**
- **4 skinless, boneless chicken breast halves**
- **1 tablespoon olive oil**
- **2 medium yellow summer squash and/or zucchini, sliced (2½ cups)**
- **1 medium green or red sweet pepper, cut into thin strips**
- **1 cup chicken broth**
- **4 teaspoons all-purpose flour**
- **1 medium tomato, seeded and cut into chunks (optional)**

1. Cook pasta according to package directions. Meanwhile, in a small bowl combine thyme, lemon-pepper seasoning, and garlic. Set aside half of the mixture. Rub remaining herb mixture into chicken.

2. In a large skillet heat oil over medium-high heat. Add chicken; reduce heat to medium. Cook for 8 to 12 minutes or until no longer pink (170°F), turning once.

3. Remove chicken from skillet; cover and keep warm. Add squash, sweet pepper, and reserved herb mixture to skillet. Cook and stir over medium heat for 3 to 4 minutes or until vegetables are crisp-tender. In a small bowl combine broth and flour. Add to skillet. Cook and stir until thick and bubbly. Cook and stir for 1 minute more.

4. Drain pasta and return to pan; add vegetable mixture and toss gently to combine. Arrange pasta mixture on dinner plates. Slice chicken and arrange on top of pasta mixture. If desired, sprinkle with tomato.

Makes 4 servings

PER SERVING: 396 cal., 6 g total fat (1 g sat. fat), 66 mg chol., 727 mg sodium, 48 g carbo., 3 g fiber, 35 g pro.

SHOPPING LIST

1 16-ounce package dried fettuccine
1 small container lemon-pepper seasoning
4 skinless, boneless chicken breast halves
2 medium yellow summer squash
1 medium green sweet pepper
1 14-ounce can chicken broth

PANTRY LIST

Dried thyme
Bottled minced garlic
Olive oil
All-purpose flour

40
MINUTES

BUFFALO CHICKEN SANDWICH

START TO FINISH: *40 minutes*

- **4 skinless, boneless chicken breast halves**
- **Salt and ground black pepper**
- **1 egg, lightly beaten**
- **1 tablespoon bottled hot pepper sauce**
- **½ cup fine dry bread crumbs**
- **2 tablespoons cooking oil**
- **4 kaiser rolls, split and toasted**
- **¼ cup bottled blue cheese salad dressing**
- **2 medium carrots, cut into bite-size sticks**
- **2 stalks celery, cut into bite-size sticks**
- **Bottled blue cheese salad dressing**
- **Bottled hot pepper sauce**

1. Place each chicken breast half between 2 pieces of plastic wrap. Using the flat side of a meat mallet, pound the boned side of chicken lightly until it is an even ½-inch thickness. Sprinkle chicken lightly with salt and pepper.

2. In a shallow dish stir together egg and 1 tablespoon hot pepper sauce. In another dish place bread crumbs. Dip chicken in egg mixture, then in crumbs to coat.

3. In a large skillet cook chicken in hot oil over medium heat for 10 to 12 minutes or until chicken is no longer pink (170°F), turning once. (Reduce heat to medium-low if chicken browns too quickly.)

4. Place 1 chicken piece on the bottom of each bun. Drizzle each with 1 tablespoon dressing. Add bun tops. Serve with carrots, celery, additional dressing, and pepper sauce.

Makes 4 servings

PER SERVING: 698 cal., 37 g total fat (7 g sat. fat), 143 mg chol., 1,249 mg sodium, 47 g carbo., 3 g fiber, 45 g pro.

SHOPPING LIST

4 skinless, boneless chicken breast halves
1 8-ounce package fine dry bread crumbs
1 package kaiser rolls
1 16-ounce bottle blue cheese salad dressing
1 1-pound bag carrots
1 bunch celery

PANTRY LIST

Salt
Ground black pepper
Egg
Cooking oil
Bottled hot pepper sauce

40 MINUTES

COCONUT CHICKEN THIGHS

START TO FINISH: *40 minutes*

- **1½ cups chicken broth**
- **2 tablespoons lime juice**
- **1 tablespoon packed brown sugar**
- **1 teaspoon grated fresh ginger**
- **1 cup uncooked basmati rice or long grain white rice**
- **1 medium red sweet pepper, cut into bite-size strips**
- **1 small onion, cut into wedges**
- **2 tablespoons cooking oil**
- **1½ pounds skinless, boneless chicken thighs**
- **¾ cup unsweetened coconut milk**
- **½ teaspoon salt**
- **⅛ teaspoon crushed red pepper**
- **¼ cup snipped fresh cilantro**

1. In a medium saucepan stir together broth, lime juice, brown sugar, and ginger. Bring to boiling. Stir in rice. Reduce heat. Simmer, covered, for 20 minutes or until rice is tender and liquid is absorbed.

2. Meanwhile, in a large skillet cook sweet pepper and onion in 1 tablespoon hot oil for 3 minutes. Remove from skillet. Add remaining 1 tablespoon oil to skillet. Add chicken. Cook for 5 to 6 minutes or until chicken is brown, turning once. Return vegetables to skillet. Add coconut milk, salt, and crushed red pepper. Bring to boiling; reduce heat. Simmer, covered, for 5 to 10 minutes or until chicken is no longer pink (180°F). Sprinkle with cilantro.

3. To serve, remove chicken and vegetables to a serving dish with rice. Drizzle with some of the cooking liquid. Pass remaining cooking liquid.

Makes 6 servings

PER SERVING: 377 cal., 16 g total fat (8 g sat. fat), 95 mg chol., 539 mg sodium, 31 g carbo., 2 g fiber, 26 g pro.

SHOPPING LIST

1 14-ounce can chicken broth
1 lime
1 piece fresh ginger
1 16-ounce package basmati or long grain rice
1 red sweet pepper
1 small onion
1½ pounds skinless, boneless chicken thighs
1 13- to 14-ounce can unsweetened coconut milk
1 bunch fresh cilantro

PANTRY LIST

Brown sugar
Cooking oil
Salt
Crushed red pepper

40
MINUTES

SKILLET CACCIATORE

START TO FINISH: *40 minutes*

- **8 ounces dried bow tie pasta (3 cups)**
- **4 skinless, boneless chicken breast halves**
- **1 tablespoon olive oil**
- **1 8-ounce package sliced mushrooms**
- **1½ cups red, green, and/or orange sweet pepper cut into bite-size strips**
- **1 medium onion, cut into thin wedges**
- **1 14-ounce can diced tomatoes with basil, garlic, and oregano, undrained**
- **1 teaspoon dried Italian seasoning, crushed**
- **¼ teaspoon crushed red pepper**
- **Finely shredded Parmesan cheese**

1. Prepare pasta according to package directions; drain.

2. Meanwhile, in a large skillet cook chicken in hot oil about 5 minutes or until brown, turning once; remove from skillet. Add mushrooms, sweet pepper, and onion to skillet. Cook over medium-high heat for 5 minutes or until tender. Stir in undrained tomatoes, Italian seasoning, and crushed red pepper. Bring to boiling. Return chicken to skillet; reduce heat. Simmer, covered, for 15 minutes or until chicken is no longer pink (170°F). Serve chicken and sauce over pasta; sprinkle with Parmesan cheese.

Makes 4 servings

PER SERVING: 476 cal., 8 g total fat (2 g sat. fat), 87 mg chol., 374 mg sodium, 55 g carbo., 5 g fiber, 45 g pro.

SHOPPING LIST

1 16-ounce package dried bow tie pasta

4 skinless, boneless chicken breast halves

1 8-ounce package sliced mushrooms

2 medium sweet peppers

1 medium onion

1 14-ounce can diced tomatoes with basil, garlic, and oregano

1 5-ounce package finely shredded Parmesan cheese

PANTRY LIST

Olive oil

Dried Italian seasoning

Crushed red pepper

40 MINUTES

TORTILLA CHICKEN SOUP

START TO FINISH: *40 minutes*

- **2** **14-ounce cans reduced-sodium chicken broth**
- **1** **10.75-ounce can condensed tomato soup**
- **1** **medium onion, chopped (½ cup)**
- **½** **cup chopped green sweet pepper**
- **4** **skinless, boneless chicken breast halves, cut into bite-size pieces**
- **1** **cup loose-pack frozen whole kernel corn**
- **1½** **teaspoons chili powder**
- **½** **teaspoon ground cumin**
- **⅛** **teaspoon ground black pepper**
- **3** **cups tortilla chips, coarsely crushed**
- **1** **cup shredded Monterey Jack cheese (4 ounces)**
- **1** **avocado, seeded, peeled, and cut up (optional)**
- **Snipped fresh cilantro (optional)**

1. In a 4-quart Dutch oven combine chicken broth, tomato soup, onion, and sweet pepper. Bring to boiling. Add chicken. Return to boiling; reduce heat. Simmer, covered, for 10 minutes.

2. Add corn, chili powder, cumin, and black pepper. Return to boiling; reduce heat. Simmer, covered, for 10 minutes more.

3. To serve, top with tortilla chips and cheese. If desired, serve with avocado and cilantro.

Makes 6 servings

PER SERVING: 318 cal., 11 g total fat (5 g sat. fat), 71 mg chol., 905 mg sodium, 24 g carbo., 3 g fiber, 31 g pro.

SHOPPING LIST

2 14-ounce cans reduced-sodium chicken broth

1 10.75-ounce can condensed tomato soup

1 medium onion

1 medium green sweet pepper

4 skinless, boneless chicken breast halves

1 10-ounce package frozen whole kernel corn

1 16-ounce package tortilla chips

1 8-ounce package shredded Monterey Jack cheese

PANTRY LIST

Chili powder

Ground cumin

Ground black pepper

40 MINUTES

QUICK CHICKEN STEW

START TO FINISH: *35 minutes*

- **3 tablespoons all-purpose flour**
- **1/8 teaspoon salt**
- **1/8 teaspoon ground black pepper**
- **4 skinless, boneless chicken breast halves, halved crosswise**
- **2 tablespoons olive oil**
- **2 cups fresh mushrooms, quartered**
- **2 tablespoons finely chopped onion**
- **1 teaspoon minced garlic**
- **6 ounces baby carrots with tops**
- **2 cups fresh green beans, cut into 2-inch lengths**
- **3/4 cup chicken broth**
- **3/4 cup dry white wine**
- **2 teaspoons lemon juice**
- **1 tablespoon snipped fresh dillweed or 1/2 teaspoon dried dillweed**

1. In a shallow bowl combine flour, salt, and pepper. Coat chicken breasts with flour mixture, shaking off excess and reserving remaining flour. In a large skillet cook chicken in hot oil for 4 minutes or until golden brown, turning once. Remove chicken; set aside.

2. Add mushrooms, onion, and garlic to skillet. Cook and stir about 3 minutes or until vegetables are tender. Meanwhile, remove all but 1 inch of carrot tops; halve carrots lengthwise and discard greens. Add carrots and beans to skillet. Sprinkle vegetables with remaining flour mixture; stir well.

3. Remove skillet from heat; stir in broth and wine. Return skillet to heat; return chicken breasts to pan. Bring mixture to boiling; reduce heat. Simmer, covered, about 5 minutes or until chicken is no longer pink (170°F). Stir in lemon juice and dillweed.

Makes 4 servings

PER SERVING: 293 cal., 10 g total fat (2 g sat. fat), 66 mg chol., 356 mg sodium, 15 g carbo., 4 g fiber, 30 g pro.

SHOPPING LIST

4 skinless, boneless chicken breast halves

1 8-ounce package fresh mushrooms

1 small onion

6 ounces fresh baby carrots

8 ounces fresh green beans

1 14-ounce can chicken broth

1 bottle dry white wine

1 lemon

1 package fresh dillweed

PANTRY LIST

All-purpose flour

Salt

Ground black pepper

Olive oil

Garlic

40
MINUTES

KALAMATA LEMON CHICKEN

START TO FINISH: *40 minutes*

- **1 to 1¼ pounds skinless, boneless chicken thighs**
- **1 tablespoon olive oil**
- **⅔ cup dried orzo**
- **½ cup pitted kalamata olives**
- **1 14-ounce can chicken broth**
- **½ of a lemon, cut into wedges**
- **1 tablespoon lemon juice**
- **1 teaspoon dried Greek seasoning**
- **¼ teaspoon salt**
- **¼ teaspoon freshly ground black pepper**
- **Hot chicken broth (optional)**
- **Fresh snipped oregano (optional)**

1. Preheat oven to 400°F. In a 4-quart Dutch oven cook chicken in hot oil over medium-high heat for 5 minutes, turning once. Stir in orzo, olives, broth, lemon wedges, lemon juice, Greek seasoning, salt, and pepper.

2. Bake, covered, for 35 minutes or until chicken is no longer pink (180°F). If desired, serve in shallow bowls with additional broth and snipped oregano.

Makes 4 servings

PER SERVING: 309 cal., 11 g total fat (2 g sat. fat), 91 mg chol., 837 mg sodium, 24 g carbo., 2 g fiber, 27 g pro.

SHOPPING LIST

1 pound skinless, boneless chicken thighs
1 8-ounce package dried orzo
1 6-ounce jar pitted kalamata olives
1 14-ounce can chicken broth
1 lemon
1 small container Greek seasoning

PANTRY LIST

Olive oil
Salt
Black pepper

40 MINUTES

CHICKEN WITH BLACK-EYED PEAS AND YELLOW RICE

START TO FINISH: *35 minutes*

- **1 cup chopped red onion**
- **1 tablespoon olive oil**
- **1½ pounds chicken breast tenderloins**
- **2 cloves garlic, minced**
- **1 14-ounce can reduced-sodium chicken broth**
- **½ teaspoon poultry seasoning**
- **¼ to ½ teaspoon ground black pepper**
- **¼ teaspoon crushed red pepper**
- **¾ cup saffron-flavor yellow rice mix***
- **1 15-ounce can black-eyed peas, rinsed and drained**
- **1 tablespoon snipped fresh thyme**

1. In an extra-large skillet cook onion in hot oil over medium heat about 4 minutes or until tender. Add chicken and garlic; cook about 4 minutes more or until chicken is brown, turning once.

2. Stir in broth, poultry seasoning, black pepper, and crushed red pepper. Bring mixture to boiling. Stir in uncooked rice. Reduce heat. Cook, covered, about 10 minutes or until rice is almost tender.

3. Stir in black-eyed peas and thyme. Cook, covered, about 10 minutes or until heated through and liquid is absorbed.

Makes 6 servings

PER SERVING: 280 cal., 4 g total fat (1 g sat. fat), 66 mg chol., 641 mg sodium, 28 g carbo., 4 g fiber, 32 g pro.

*Note: You can find saffron-flavor yellow rice mix with other rice mixes in the supermarket. Look for a brand that combines the seasonings and the rice. If the brand comes with a separate seasoning packet, mix the seasonings with the rice in a separate bowl and measure out ¾ cup.

SHOPPING LIST

1 large red onion
1½ pounds chicken breast tenderloins
1 14-ounce can reduced-sodium chicken broth
1 small container poultry seasoning
1 8-ounce package saffron-flavor yellow rice mix
1 15-ounce can black-eyed peas
1 package fresh thyme

PANTRY LIST

Olive oil
Garlic
Ground black pepper
Crushed red pepper

40
MINUTES

CHICKEN AND BISCUITS

START TO FINISH: *40 minutes*

- **1 cup packaged biscuit mix**
- **¼ cup shredded cheddar cheese**
- **1 tablespoon chopped fresh parsley**
- **⅓ cup milk**
- **1 purchased roasted chicken**
- **1 medium onion, chopped**
- **2 tablespoons butter**
- **2 tablespoons all-purpose flour**
- **½ teaspoon dried thyme, crushed**
- **¼ teaspoon ground black pepper**
- **1 14-ounce can chicken broth**
- **1 15-ounce can large-cut mixed vegetables, drained**
- **½ cup milk**

1. Preheat oven to 400°F. Grease a large baking sheet; set aside. In a medium bowl combine biscuit mix, cheese, parsley, and ⅓ cup milk. Spoon into 4 mounds on prepared baking sheet. Bake for 10 to 12 minutes or until bottoms are light brown.

2. Meanwhile, remove 3 cups meat from chicken and coarsely chop. Reserve remaining chicken for another use.

3. In a large skillet cook onion in hot butter over medium heat for 5 minutes or until tender. Stir in flour, thyme, and pepper. Add broth all at once. Cook and stir until thick and bubbly. Stir in chicken, vegetables, and ½ cup milk.

4. Divide chicken mixture among 4 shallow bowls. Serve with warm biscuits.

Makes 4 servings

PER SERVING: 495 cal., 22 g total fat (9 g sat. fat), 122 mg chol., 1,220 mg sodium, 33 g carbo., 5 g fiber, 39 g pro.

SHOPPING LIST

1 20-ounce box biscuit mix
1 8-ounce package shredded cheddar cheese
1 bunch fresh parsley
1 purchased roasted chicken
1 medium onion
1 14-ounce can chicken broth
1 15-ounce can large-cut mixed vegetables

PANTRY LIST

Milk
Butter
All-purpose flour
Dried thyme
Ground black pepper

40 MINUTES

OVEN BARBECUE CHICKEN

START TO FINISH: *40 minutes*

- **4 skinless, boneless chicken breast halves**
- **1 tablespoon barbecue spice**
- **¼ cup butter, melted**
- **¾ cup finely crushed cornflakes**
- **1 15-ounce can black beans, rinsed and drained**
- **1 11-ounce can whole kernel corn with sweet peppers, drained**
- **1 medium tomato, chopped**
- **1 jalapeño pepper, finely chopped* (optional)**
- **1 tablespoon lime juice**
- **1 teaspoon ground cumin**
- **2 jalapeño peppers, halved lengthwise and broiled (optional)**

1. Preheat oven to 375°F. Lightly grease a baking sheet; set aside. Sprinkle both sides of chicken with barbecue spice. Place butter in a shallow dish; dip chicken in butter to coat. Place cornflakes in a resealable plastic bag. Add chicken breast halves to the bag one at a time; seal bag and shake to coat. Place chicken on prepared baking sheet. Sprinkle chicken with any remaining crushed cornflakes.

2. Bake for 20 to 25 minutes or until chicken is no longer pink (170°F). Meanwhile, in a medium bowl combine black beans, corn, tomato, chopped jalapeño (if desired), lime juice, and cumin. Serve salsa with chicken and, if desired, broiled jalapeños.

Makes 4 servings

PER SERVING: 448 cal., 14 g total fat (8 g sat. fat), 113 mg chol., 1,658 mg sodium, 45 g carbo., 8 g fiber, 41 g pro.

*Note: Because hot chile peppers, such as jalapeños, contain volatile oils that can burn your skin and eyes, avoid direct contact with chiles as much as possible. When working with chile peppers, wear plastic or rubber gloves. If your bare hands do touch the chile peppers, wash your hands well with soap and water.

SHOPPING LIST

4 skinless, boneless chicken breast halves

1 small container barbecue spice

1 18-ounce box cornflakes

1 15-ounce can black beans

3 jalapeño peppers

1 11-ounce can whole kernel corn with sweet peppers

1 medium tomato

1 lime

PANTRY LIST

Butter

Ground cumin

40
MINUTES

TURKEY AND SWEET POTATOES

START TO FINISH: *40 minutes*

- **1 pound sweet potatoes**
- **2 turkey breast tenderloins (1 to 1¼ pounds)**
- **½ teaspoon salt**
- **¼ teaspoon ground black pepper**
- **1 tablespoon cooking oil**
- **1 cup purchased chunky salsa**
- **¼ cup orange juice**
- **Snipped fresh cilantro or parsley (optional)**

1. Peel potatoes; cut into 1-inch pieces. In a saucepan cook sweet potatoes, covered, in enough boiling water to cover for 10 to 12 minutes or until potatoes are just tender; drain.

2. Meanwhile, cut turkey crosswise into ½-inch slices. Sprinkle with salt and pepper. In a large nonstick skillet cook turkey in hot oil over medium-high heat for 3 to 4 minutes per side or until turkey is no longer pink.

3. Add salsa and orange juice to skillet; add sweet potatoes. Cook until heated through, stirring gently. If desired, sprinkle with snipped fresh cilantro.

Makes 4 servings

PER SERVING: 251 cal., 4 g total fat (1 g sat. fat), 70 mg chol., 775 mg sodium, 22 g carbo., 7 g fiber, 30 g pro.

SHOPPING LIST

1 pound sweet potatoes
2 turkey breast tenderloins
1 16-ounce jar chunky salsa

PANTRY LIST

Salt
Ground black pepper
Cooking oil
Orange juice

40
MINUTES

TASTY TURKEY CHILI

START TO FINISH: *40 minutes*

- **1¼ pounds uncooked ground turkey**
- **2 large onions, chopped (2 cups)**
- **¼ cup water**
- **2 cloves garlic, minced**
- **1 15-ounce can tomato sauce**
- **1 14.5-ounce can tomatoes, cut up, undrained**
- **1 cup water**
- **1 tablespoon chili powder**
- **1 teaspoon ground cumin**
- **½ teaspoon sugar**
- **1 15-ounce can pinto beans, rinsed and drained**
- **1 cup frozen whole kernel corn**
- **1 cup shredded cheddar cheese (4 ounces)**

1. In a large saucepan cook ground turkey until no longer pink; drain. Stir in onions, the ¼ cup water, and garlic. Cook about 5 minutes more or until onion is tender, stirring often. Stir in tomato sauce, undrained tomatoes, the 1 cup water, chili powder, cumin, and sugar. Bring to boiling; reduce heat. Cover and simmer for 20 minutes, stirring occasionally.

2. Stir in beans and corn. Return to boiling; reduce heat. Cover and simmer for 10 minutes more, stirring occasionally. Ladle into bowls; sprinkle with cheese.

Makes 6 servings

PER SERVING: 342 cal., 12 g total fat (4 g sat. fat), 88 mg chol., 822 mg sodium, 30 g carbo., 7 g fiber, 30 g pro.

SHOPPING LIST

1¼ pounds uncooked ground turkey
2 large onions
1 15-ounce can tomato sauce
1 14.5-ounce can tomatoes
1 15-ounce can pinto beans
1 10-ounce package frozen whole kernel corn
1 8-ounce package shredded cheddar cheese

PANTRY LIST

Garlic
Chili powder
Ground cumin
Sugar

40
MINUTES

SAUSAGE-PEPPER MEDLEY

START TO FINISH: *40 minutes*

- **6 uncooked turkey Italian sausage links (about 1½ pounds)**
- **2 cloves garlic, minced**
- **1 tablespoon olive oil**
- **4 medium red, green, and/or yellow sweet peppers, seeded and cut into thin strips**
- **1 large onion, thinly sliced and separated into rings**
- **1 14.5-ounce can diced tomatoes, undrained**
- **1½ teaspoons dried Italian seasoning, crushed**
- **¼ teaspoon crushed red pepper (optional)**
- **⅓ cup shredded Parmesan cheese**

1. In an extra-large nonstick skillet cook sausage over medium heat for 5 to 8 minutes or until brown, turning frequently. Reduce heat to medium-low. Cook, covered, about 10 minutes more or until juices run clear. Remove sausage links from skillet; thinly bias-slice. Set aside.

2. In same skillet cook garlic in hot olive oil over medium heat for 30 seconds. Add peppers and onion; cook about 5 minutes or until crisp tender, stirring occasionally.

3. Add sausage, undrained tomatoes, Italian seasoning, and, if desired, crushed red pepper to skillet. Bring to boiling; reduce heat. Simmer, uncovered, for 5 minutes. Sprinkle with cheese.

Makes 6 servings

PER SERVING: 269 cal., 15 g total fat (4 g sat. fat), 74 mg chol., 1,123 mg sodium, 11 g carbo., 3 g fiber, 23 g pro.

SHOPPING LIST

6 uncooked turkey Italian sausage links
4 medium red sweet peppers
1 large onion
1 14.5-ounce can diced tomatoes
1 8-ounce package shredded Parmesan cheese

PANTRY LIST

Garlic
Olive oil
Dried Italian seasoning
Crushed red pepper

40
MINUTES

BALSAMIC-GLAZED SIRLOIN KABOBS

START TO FINISH: *40 minutes*

- **½ cup balsamic vinegar**
- **1 clove garlic, minced**
- **1 pound boneless beef sirloin steak, trimmed and cut into 1-inch pieces**
- **2 small red sweet peppers, seeded and cut into 1-inch pieces**
- **½ of a large sweet onion, cut into 1-inch pieces**
- **1 teaspoon dried Italian seasoning, crushed**
- **½ teaspoon salt**
- **¼ teaspoon ground black pepper**
- **1 14.8-ounce pouch cooked long grain white rice**
- **¼ cup sliced green onions**

SHOPPING LIST

1 pound boneless beef sirloin steak
2 small red sweet peppers
1 large sweet onion
1 14.8-ounce pouch cooked long grain rice
1 bunch green onions

PANTRY LIST

Balsamic vinegar
Garlic
Dried Italian seasoning
Salt
Ground black pepper

1. In a small saucepan bring vinegar and garlic to boiling. Reduce heat; boil gently, uncovered, for 8 to 10 minutes or until mixture is reduced to 3 tablespoons. Remove from heat. Set aside.

2. In a large bowl combine beef, sweet peppers, and sweet onion pieces. Add Italian seasoning, salt, and black pepper; toss to coat. Thread beef, sweet peppers, and sweet onion pieces on 12-inch skewers.*

3. Place kabobs on the unheated rack of a broiler pan. Broil 3 to 4 inches from the heat for 8 to 10 minutes or until beef is desired doneness and vegetables are crisp-tender, turning kabobs once during broiling. Brush vinegar mixture over kabobs just before serving.

4. Meanwhile, heat rice according to package directions. Stir in green onion; season to taste with salt and pepper. Serve with kabobs.

Makes 4 servings

PER SERVING: 371 cal., 7 g total fat (2 g sat. fat), 48 mg chol., 510 mg sodium, 43 g carbo., 2 g fiber, 29 g pro.

*Tip: If using wooden or bamboo skewers, soak them in water for 30 minutes before using.

40 MINUTES

PEPPERCORN STEAKS

START TO FINISH: *35 minutes*

- **2 6-ounce boneless beef ribeye steaks or beef top sirloin steaks, cut about 1 inch thick**
- **1 tablespoon multicolor peppercorns, crushed**
- **½ teaspoon salt**
- **2 tablespoons butter, softened**
- **2 teaspoons mild-flavor molasses**
- **¼ teaspoon finely shredded lemon peel**
- **1 teaspoon lemon juice**
- **2 cups sugar snap peas**
- **½ cup thin bite-size strips carrot**

1. Trim fat from steaks. Using your fingers, press crushed peppercorns and salt onto both sides of each steak.

2. Place steaks on the unheated rack of a broiler pan. Broil 3 to 4 inches from the heat until desired doneness, turning once halfway through broiling time. For ribeye steaks, allow 12 to 14 minutes for medium rare (145°F) or 15 to 18 minutes for medium (160°F). For sirloin steaks, allow 15 to 17 minutes for medium rare (145°F) or 20 to 22 minutes for medium (160°F).

3. Meanwhile, in a small bowl combine butter, molasses, lemon peel, and lemon juice (mixture will appear curdled). Set aside.

4. Remove strings and tips from peas. In a medium saucepan cook peas and carrot, covered, in a small amount of boiling salted water for 2 to 4 minutes or until crisp-tender. Drain well. Stir in 1 tablespoon of the molasses mixture.

5. To serve, dot remaining molasses mixture evenly over steaks. Slice steaks and toss with vegetable mixture.

Makes 4 servings

PER SERVING: 247 cal., 12 g total fat (6 g sat. fat), 66 mg chol., 418 mg sodium, 13 g carbo., 3 g fiber, 20 g pro.

SHOPPING LIST

2 6-ounce boneless beef ribeye steaks

1 small container multicolor peppercorns

1 12-ounce bottle mild-flavor molasses

1 lemon

6 ounces fresh sugar snap peas

1 carrot

PANTRY LIST

Salt

Butter

40 MINUTES

BEEF AND VEGETABLES WITH SPAGHETTI

START TO FINISH: *35 minutes*

- **4 ounces dried whole grain or whole wheat spaghetti, broken in half**
- **12 ounces boneless beef sirloin steak**
- **1 teaspoon salt**
- **½ teaspoon freshly ground black pepper**
- **1 tablespoon olive oil**
- **1 medium onion, cut into thin wedges**
- **4 cloves garlic, minced**
- **¼ teaspoon crushed red pepper**
- **1 14.5-ounce can diced tomatoes with basil, garlic, and oregano, undrained**
- **1 cup bottled roasted red sweet peppers, drained and coarsely chopped**
- **1 tablespoon balsamic vinegar**
- **2 cups fresh baby arugula or spinach leaves**
- **1 tablespoon snipped fresh (flat-leaf) parsley**
- **1 ounce Romano cheese, shaved**

1. Cook pasta according to package directions. Drain; return pasta to hot pan. Cover and keep warm. Meanwhile, trim fat from steak. Thinly slice meat across the grain. Toss meat slices with salt and black pepper.

2. In a large skillet cook meat in hot oil over medium-high heat for 3 to 4 minutes or until desired doneness. Using a slotted spoon, remove meat from skillet; set aside. Add onion, garlic, and crushed red pepper to skillet. Cook about 5 minutes or until onion is tender, stirring occasionally.

3. Stir meat, undrained tomatoes, roasted red peppers, and balsamic vinegar into onion mixture in skillet. Heat through. Add meat mixture, arugula, and parsley to hot pasta; toss to combine.

4. To serve, divide pasta mixture among 4 shallow bowls. Top with Romano cheese.

Makes 4 servings

PER SERVING: 324 cal., 8 g total fat (2 g sat. fat), 57 mg chol., 1,122 mg sodium, 38 g carbo., 2 g fiber, 26 g pro.

SHOPPING LIST

1 16-ounce package dried whole grain spaghetti
12 ounces boneless beef sirloin steak
1 medium onion
1 14.5-ounce can diced tomatoes with basil, garlic, and oregano
1 7-ounce jar roasted red sweet peppers
1 8-ounce package baby arugula
1 bunch fresh (flat-leaf) parsley
1 piece Romano cheese

PANTRY LIST

Salt
Black pepper
Olive oil
Garlic
Crushed red pepper
Balsamic vinegar

40 MINUTES

SMOKY DOUBLE CHEESEBURGER

START TO FINISH: *40 minutes*

- **1 egg, lightly beaten**
- **½ cup soft bread crumbs**
- **3 ounces smoked cheddar cheese or cheddar cheese, finely shredded (¾ cup)**
- **3 green onions, chopped**
- **2 tablespoons Worcestershire sauce**
- **1 tablespoon Dijon-style mustard**
- **¼ teaspoon ground black pepper**
- **1¼ pounds ground beef round or ground sirloin**
- **4 onion slices (optional)**
- **4 hamburger buns, split and toasted**
- **¼ cup mango chutney or cranberry relish**
- **½ cup arugula leaves or watercress**
- **1 to 2 ounces Asiago or Parmesan cheese, shaved**

1. In a large bowl combine egg, bread crumbs, smoked cheddar, green onions, Worcestershire sauce, mustard, and pepper. Add ground beef; mix gently. Firmly shape into four 12-inch-thick patties; set aside.

2. Heat a nonstick or well-seasoned grill pan over medium-high heat until hot. Reduce heat to medium; add onion slices, if using, to grill pan. Grill for 6 to 8 minutes or until tender and light brown, turning once. Remove from pan. Add patties to pan. Cook for 9 to 12 minutes or until meat is done (160°F), turning once.

3. Spread bottoms of hamburger buns with chutney; top with arugula, patties, onion slices, if using, and shaved cheese. Add bun tops.

Makes 4 servings

PER SERVING: 586 cal., 31 g total fat (14 g sat. fat), 172 mg chol., 777 mg sodium, 35 g carbo., 2 g fiber, 41 g pro.

SHOPPING LIST

1 loaf bread
1 8-ounce package smoked cheddar cheese
1 bunch green onions
1¼ pounds ground beef round
1 large onion
1 package hamburger buns
1 12-ounce jar mango chutney
1 8-ounce package arugula leaves
1 piece Asiago cheese

PANTRY LIST

Egg
Worcestershire sauce
Dijon-style mustard
Ground black pepper

40
MINUTES

PASTA WITH BABY SALISBURY STEAKS

START TO FINISH: *40 minutes*

- **Nonstick cooking spray**
- **8 ounces mafalda or tagliatelle**
- **2 slices raisin bread or cinnamon-raisin bread, torn into small pieces**
- **¼ cup milk**
- **1 pound lean ground beef**
- **½ cup finely chopped onion**
- **1 egg, lightly beaten**
- **½ teaspoon dried oregano, crushed**
- **¼ teaspoon salt**
- **2 cups sliced zucchini and/or summer squash**
- **1 tablespoon olive oil**
- **1 26-ounce jar pasta sauce**
- **Finely shredded Parmesan cheese (optional)**

1. Preheat broiler. Lightly coat the unheated rack of a broiler pan with nonstick cooking spray; set aside. In a large saucepan cook pasta according to package directions. Drain pasta; set aside.

2. Meanwhile, in a large bowl stir together bread and milk; let stand for 5 minutes. Add ground beef, onion, egg, oregano, and salt. Mix well. Place a piece of waxed paper on a large cutting board. Pat meat mixture into a 8×6-inch rectangle on the waxed paper. Invert cutting board onto prepared rack of broiler pan. Discard waxed paper.

3. Broil meat mixture 4 to 5 inches from the heat about 20 minutes, turning once, or until meat is no longer pink (160°F). Using a long sharp knife, cut into four 4×3-inch rectangles. Cut each rectangle diagonally forming 2 triangles.

4. In the pasta pan cook squash in hot oil for 2 to 3 minutes or until crisp-tender. Stir in pasta sauce and pasta and heat through. Serve steaks with pasta mixture. If desired, sprinkle each serving with cheese.

Makes 4 servings

PER SERVING: 618 cal., 20 g total fat (7 g sat. fat), 131 mg chol., 1,254 mg sodium, 76 g carbo., 8 g fiber, 37 g pro.

SHOPPING LIST	*PANTRY LIST*
1 16-ounce package mafalda	*Nonstick cooking spray*
2 slices raisin bread	*Milk*
1 pound lean ground beef	*Egg*
1 medium onion	*Dried oregano*
2 medium zucchini	*Salt*
1 26-ounce jar pasta sauce	*Olive oil*

40
MINUTES

SIRLOIN STROGANOFF

START TO FINISH: *40 minutes*

- **1 20-ounce package refrigerated red potato wedges**
- **1 large onion, chopped (1 cup)**
- **3 cloves garlic, minced**
- **2 tablespoons butter**
- **12 to 16 ounces boneless beef sirloin steak, thinly sliced into bite-size strips**
- **4 small apples, halved and, if desired, cored, or 2 large apples, quartered**
- **1 cup apple cider**
- **1 8-ounce carton dairy sour cream**
- **¼ teaspoon salt**
- **¼ teaspoon ground black pepper**

SHOPPING LIST

1 20-ounce package refrigerated red potato wedges
1 large onion
12 ounces boneless beef sirloin steak
4 small apples
1 32-ounce bottle apple cider
1 8-ounce carton dairy sour cream

PANTRY LIST

Garlic
Butter
Salt
Ground black pepper

1. In an extra-large skillet cook potatoes, onion, and garlic in hot butter over medium-high heat for 8 minutes or until nearly tender. Stir in beef strips. Cook and stir for 3 minutes more or until meat is desired doneness; remove meat and potatoes to plate. Cover; keep warm.

2. In the same skillet cook apples, cut sides down, in drippings for 2 minutes or until brown. Stir in apple cider. Bring to boiling; reduce heat. Simmer, covered, for 6 to 8 minutes or until tender. Use a slotted spoon to transfer apples from skillet to plate. Cover; keep warm.

3. Remove skillet from heat. For sauce, whisk sour cream, salt, and pepper into juices in skillet until smooth. Spoon sauce over meat, potatoes, and apples.

Makes 4 servings

PER SERVING: 538 cal., 25 g total fat (14 g sat. fat), 82 mg chol., 359 mg sodium, 51 g carbo., 5 g fiber, 22 g pro.

40 MINUTES

POLENTA WITH ITALIAN BEEF STEW

START TO FINISH: *40 minutes*

- **1 pound lean ground beef**
- **1 14.5-ounce can diced tomatoes with basil, garlic, and oregano**
- **3 medium carrots, cut into ½-inch slices**
- **2 medium onions, cut into thin wedges**
- **1 large red sweet pepper, cut into 1-inch pieces**
- **½ cup beef broth**
- **3 tablespoons tomato paste**
- **¼ teaspoon salt**
- **¼ teaspoon ground black pepper**
- **1 teaspoon bottled minced garlic**
- **1 medium zucchini, halved lengthwise and cut into ¼-inch slices**
- **⅓ cup purchased basil pesto**
- **1 16-ounce tube refrigerated cooked polenta**

1. In a large skillet cook ground beef over medium heat until brown. Drain off fat. Stir in undrained tomatoes, carrots, onions, sweet pepper, beef broth, tomato paste, salt, black pepper, and garlic. Bring to boiling; reduce heat. Cover and simmer for 10 to 15 minutes or until carrots are tender. Stir in zucchini and pesto. Cover and simmer for 5 minutes more.

2. Meanwhile, prepare polenta according to package directions. Serve meat mixture with polenta.

Makes 6 servings

PER SERVING: 362 cal., 16 g total fat (3 g sat. fat), 50 mg chol., 978 mg sodium, 34 g carbo., 5 g fiber, 20 g pro.

SHOPPING LIST

1 pound lean ground beef
1 14.5-ounce can diced tomatoes with basil, garlic, and oregano
1 package carrots
2 medium onions
1 large red sweet pepper
1 14-ounce can beef broth
1 6-ounce can tomato paste
1 medium zucchini
1 4-ounce jar basil pesto
1 16-ounce tube refrigerated cooked polenta

PANTRY LIST

Salt
Ground black pepper
Bottled minced garlic

40 MINUTES

SOFT-SHELL BURRITOS

START TO FINISH: *35 minutes*

- **6** **8-inch flour tortillas**
- **12** **ounces ground beef**
- **½** **cup chopped onion (1 medium)**
- **2** **cloves garlic, minced**
- **½** **cup chopped green sweet pepper (1 small)**
- **½** **cup bottled salsa or picante sauce**
- **2** **teaspoons Mexican seasoning**
- **1½** **cups shredded lettuce**
- **1** **cup chopped tomatoes (2 medium)**
- **½** **cup shredded cheddar or Monterey Jack cheese (2 ounces)**
- **Shredded cheddar or Monterey Jack cheese**
- **Bottled salsa or picante sauce (optional)**

1. Wrap tortillas in foil; bake in a 350°F oven about 10 minutes or until warm.

2. Meanwhile, in a large skillet cook ground beef, onion, and garlic over medium-high heat until meat is brown and onion is tender. Drain off fat. Stir in sweet pepper, ½ cup salsa, and Mexican seasoning. Bring to boiling; reduce heat. Simmer, covered, for 10 minutes.

3. Place tortillas on work surface. Top each tortilla with about ½ cup of the meat mixture and some of the lettuce and tomatoes. Sprinkle with the ½ cup cheese. Fold in sides; roll up. Cut in half to serve. If desired, sprinkle with additional cheese and pass additional salsa.

Makes 6 servings

PER SERVING: 252 cal., 7 g total fat (3 g sat. fat), 42 mg chol., 532 mg sodium, 29 g carbo., 2 g fiber, 16 g pro.

SHOPPING LIST

1 package 8-inch flour tortillas
12 ounces ground beef
1 medium onion
1 small green sweet pepper
1 8-ounce bottle salsa
1 small container Mexican seasoning
1 head lettuce
2 medium tomatoes
1 8-ounce package shredded cheddar cheese

PANTRY LIST

Garlic

40
MINUTES

TACO SHEPHERD'S PIE

START TO FINISH: *40 minutes*

1 18-ounce package taco sauce with seasoned ground beef

1 24-ounce package refrigerated country-style mashed potatoes

1 15-ounce can black beans, rinsed and drained

1 11-ounce can whole kernel corn with sweet peppers, drained

1 14.5-ounce can Mexican-style stewed tomatoes, drained

1 4-ounce can diced green chiles

1 cup shredded Mexican-style four-cheese blend

Dairy sour cream (optional)

1. Preheat oven to 400°F. Heat taco meat and mashed potatoes according to package directions. Stir beans and corn into taco meat. Stir drained tomatoes and green chiles into mashed potatoes.

2. Spoon meat mixture into a 2-quart square baking dish. Spoon mashed potato mixture in mounds over meat mixture. Sprinkle cheese over potatoes. Bake, uncovered, for 20 minutes or until mixture is bubbly. If desired, top each serving with sour cream.

Makes 6 servings

PER SERVING: 401 cal., 15 g total fat (7 g sat. fat), 39 mg chol., 1,624 mg sodium, 47 g carbo., 7 g fiber, 20 g pro.

SHOPPING LIST

1 18-ounce package taco sauce with seasoned ground beef

1 24-ounce package refrigerated country-style mashed potatoes

1 15-ounce can black beans

1 14.5-ounce can Mexican-style stewed tomatoes

1 11-ounce can whole kernel corn with sweet peppers

1 4-ounce can diced green chiles

1 8-ounce package shredded Mexican-style four-cheese blend

40
MINUTES

FIRE-AND-SPICE BEEF BURGERS

START TO FINISH: *35 minutes*

- **1 egg, lightly beaten**
- **¾ cup soft bread crumbs (1 slice)**
- **⅓ cup finely chopped onion**
- **2 tablespoons plain yogurt**
- **½ teaspoon salt**
- **½ teaspoon ground cinnamon or ground cardamom**
- **½ teaspoon ground coriander or mace**
- **¼ teaspoon cayenne pepper**
- **1 pound ground beef, lamb, or pork**
- **¼ cup jalapeño or hot pepper jelly**
- **4 lettuce leaves**
- **2 large pita bread rounds, halved crosswise**

1. Preheat broiler. In a large bowl combine egg and bread crumbs. Stir in onion, yogurt, salt, cinnamon, coriander, and cayenne pepper. Add ground meat; mix well. Shape mixture into 4 oval patties about 5 inches long and ½ inch thick.

2. Place patties on the unheated rack of a broiler pan. Broil 3 to 4 inches from the heat for 11 to 13 minutes or until done (160°F), turning halfway through broiling time, and brushing once with 2 tablespoons of the jelly. Spoon remaining jelly over patties before serving. Serve burgers in lettuce-lined pita halves.

Makes 4 servings

PER SERVING: 410 cal., 16 g total fat (6 g sat. fat), 125 mg chol., 585 mg sodium, 37 g carbo., 2 g fiber, 28 g pro.

SHOPPING LIST

1 loaf bread
1 small onion
1 6-ounce container plain yogurt
1 small container coriander
1 pound ground beef
1 10-ounce jar jalapeño jelly
1 head lettuce
1 package large pita bread rounds

PANTRY LIST

Egg
Salt
Ground cinnamon
Cayenne pepper

40
MINUTES

PORK TENDERLOIN WITH CREAMY MUSTARD SAUCE

START TO FINISH: *40 minutes*

- **1 1-pound pork tenderloin, trimmed**
- **Nonstick cooking spray**
- **Salt and ground black pepper**
- **¼ cup finely chopped shallots or onion**
- **1 clove garlic, minced**
- **1 tablespoon olive oil**
- **¼ cup beef broth**
- **1 to 2 tablespoons Dijon-style mustard**
- **¼ teaspoon dried thyme, crushed**
- **1 cup whipping cream**

1. Place tenderloin in a ungreased 13×9×2-inch baking pan. Lightly coat tenderloin with cooking spray and sprinkle with salt and pepper. Roast, uncovered, in a 425°F oven for 25 to 30 minutes or until juices run clear (155°F). Cover with foil; let stand for 10 minutes. (The temperature of the meat after standing should be 160°F.)

2. Meanwhile, in a medium skillet cook shallots and garlic in hot oil for 3 to 4 minutes or until tender. Add broth; simmer, uncovered, until most of the liquid evaporates. Stir in Dijon-style mustard and thyme. Stir in cream; simmer, uncovered, for 4 to 5 minutes or until thickened to desired consistency. Serve sauce over pork.

Makes 4 servings

PER SERVING: 386 cal., 30 g total fat (16 g sat. fat), 156 mg chol., 372 mg sodium, 4 g carbo., 0 g fiber, 25 g pro.

SHOPPING LIST

1 1-pound pork tenderloin
2 medium shallots
1 14-ounce can beef broth
1 8-ounce container whipping cream

PANTRY LIST

Nonstick cooking spray
Salt
Ground black pepper
Garlic
Olive oil
Dijon-style mustard
Dried thyme

40
MINUTES

MEXI-PORK WRAPS

START TO FINISH: *35 minutes*

- **8 ounces lean boneless pork, cut into thin bite-size strips**
- **1 clove garlic, minced**
- **1 tablespoon olive oil**
- **¾ cup frozen whole kernel corn, thawed**
- **½ cup chopped roasted red sweet peppers**
- **¼ cup sliced green onions (2)**
- **3 tablespoons lime juice**
- **½ teaspoon ground cumin**
- **⅛ teaspoon cayenne pepper (optional)**
- **½ cup refried black beans***
- **4 9- or 10-inch whole grain tortillas**
- **½ cup shredded romaine**
- **½ cup chopped tomatoes**
- **Light dairy sour cream (optional)**

1. In a large skillet cook and stir pork strips and garlic in hot oil over medium-high heat for 4 to 5 minutes or until no pink remains; set aside.

2. In a medium bowl stir together corn, roasted sweet peppers, green onions, 2 tablespoons of the lime juice, cumin, and, if desired, cayenne pepper. In a small bowl stir together refried beans and remaining 1 tablespoon lime juice.

3. Spread 2 tablespoons of black bean mixture in a 2-inch-wide strip in the center of each tortilla. Top with pork strips, corn mixture, romaine, and tomatoes. Fold bottom edge of each tortilla over the filling. Roll up tortillas around filling. If desired, serve with sour cream.

Makes 4 wraps

PER WRAP: 316 cal., 11 g total fat (3 g sat. fat), 36 mg chol., 484 mg sodium, 39 g carbo., 5 g fiber, 17 g pro.

MEXI-CHICKEN WRAPS: Prepare as above, except substitute skinless, boneless chicken breast halves, cut into bite-size strips, for the pork.

*Note: If you can't find refried black beans, rinse and drain ½ of a 15-ounce can black beans. In a small bowl mash beans; stir in 1 tablespoon lime juice.

SHOPPING LIST

8 ounces boneless pork
1 10-ounce package frozen whole kernel corn
1 7-ounce jar roasted red sweet peppers
1 bunch green onions
1 8-ounce bottle lime juice
1 16-ounce can refried black beans
1 package whole grain tortillas
1 head romaine
1 large fresh tomato

PANTRY LIST

Garlic
Olive oil
Ground cumin
Cayenne pepper

40
MINUTES

PORK AND CHORIZO STEW

START TO FINISH: *40 minutes*

- **1** **1-pound pork tenderloin, cut into 1-inch cubes**
- **8** **ounces cooked smoked chorizo sausage, cut into ¼-inch slices**
- **1** **tablespoon cooking oil**
- **1** **cup coarsely chopped onion (1 large)**
- **2** **cloves garlic, minced**
- **2** **tablespoons all-purpose flour**
- **½** **teaspoon dried thyme, crushed**
- **2½** **cups reduced-sodium beef broth**
- **1** **cup frozen peas and carrots**
- **Salt and ground black pepper**
- **2** **cups dried egg noodles**

1. In a 4-quart Dutch oven cook pork cubes and chorizo in hot oil over medium-high heat for 10 minutes or until brown. Using a slotted spoon, transfer meat to a plate; set aside.

2. Add onion and garlic to pan. Cook and stir for 4 to 5 minutes or until tender. Return meat and any accumulated juices to pan. Add flour and thyme. Cook and stir for 1 minute.

3. Gradually add broth, stirring to loosen any browned bits from bottom of pan. Add frozen peas and carrots. Bring to boiling; reduce heat. Simmer, uncovered, for 15 to 20 minutes. Season to taste with salt and pepper.

4. Meanwhile, in a large pan cook egg noodles according to package directions. Drain well. Serve stew with noodles.

Makes 4 servings

PER SERVING: 555 cal., 30 g total fat (10 g sat. fat), 140 mg chol., 1,211 mg sodium, 26 g carbo., 3 g fiber, 43 g pro.

SHOPPING LIST

1 1-pound pork tenderloin

8 ounces cooked smoked chorizo sausage

1 large onion

2 14-ounce cans reduced-sodium beef broth

1 16-ounce package frozen peas and carrots

1 16-ounce package dried egg noodles

PANTRY LIST

Cooking oil

Garlic

All-purpose flour

Dried thyme

Salt

Ground black pepper

40
MINUTES

ASIAN PORK TENDERLOIN WITH RAMEN NOODLE SALAD

START TO FINISH: *35 minutes*

1 12- to 16-ounce pork tenderloin
Salt and ground black pepper
1 3-ounce package ramen noodles (any flavor)
2 tablespoons cooking oil
¼ cup bottled plum sauce
1 tablespoon soy sauce
½ cup thinly sliced bok choy
½ cup packaged coarsely shredded fresh carrot
⅓ cup bias-sliced green onions
½ of a small red sweet pepper, cut into thin strips
¼ cup lightly packed cilantro leaves
⅓ cup bottled light ginger vinaigrette salad dressing

1. Cut tenderloin into ½-inch slices. Place each slice between 2 sheets of plastic wrap; with the flat side of a meat mallet pound to ¼ inch thick. Sprinkle lightly with salt and black pepper. Set aside.

2. Discard seasoning packet from noodles. Cook noodles according to package directions; drain. Rinse with cold water; drain again. Snip noodles a few times with clean kitchen scissors.

3. Meanwhile, in a very large skillet heat oil over medium-high heat. Add half of the tenderloin slices; reduce heat to medium. Cook about 2 minutes per side or until barely pink in center. Remove; cook remaining pork. Return all pork to skillet. Add plum sauce and soy sauce, turning meat to coat. Remove from skillet.

4. For salad, in a serving bowl combine ramen noodles, bok choy, carrot, green onions, sweet pepper, and cilantro. Add salad dressing and toss to combine. Serve salad with pork.

Makes 4 servings

PER SERVING: 352 cal., 17 g total fat (4 g sat. fat), 55 mg chol., 1,182 mg sodium, 29 g carbo., 2 g fiber, 21 g pro.

SHOPPING LIST

1 12- to 16-ounce pork tenderloin
1 3-ounce package ramen noodles (any flavor)
1 5.5-ounce jar plum sauce
1 bunch bok choy
1 16-ounce bag shredded carrots
1 bunch green onions
1 small red sweet pepper
1 bunch fresh cilantro
1 16-ounce bottle light ginger vinaigrette salad dressing

PANTRY LIST

Salt
Ground black pepper
Soy sauce
Cooking oil

40
MINUTES

SPICY SKILLET PORK CHOPS

START TO FINISH: *40 minutes*

- **1½ cups frozen whole kernel corn**
- **1 10-ounce can chopped tomatoes and green chile peppers, undrained**
- **½ teaspoon ground cumin**
- **¼ teaspoon bottled hot pepper sauce**
- **2 cloves garlic, minced**
- **4 boneless pork loin chops, cut ¾ inch thick**
- **½ teaspoon chili powder**
- **2 teaspoons cooking oil**
- **1 medium onion, cut into thin wedges**
- **1 tablespoon snipped fresh cilantro**

SHOPPING LIST

1 10-ounce package frozen whole kernel corn
1 10-ounce can chopped tomatoes and green chile peppers
4 boneless pork loin chops
1 medium onion
1 bunch fresh cilantro

PANTRY LIST

Ground cumin
Bottled hot pepper sauce
Garlic
Chili powder
Cooking oil

1. In a medium bowl combine corn, undrained tomatoes, cumin, hot pepper sauce, and garlic; set aside.

2. Trim fat from chops. Sprinkle both sides of each chop with chili powder. In an extra-large nonstick skillet cook chops in hot oil over medium-high heat about 4 minutes or until brown, turning once. Remove chops from skillet, reserving drippings. Reduce heat to medium. Add onion to skillet; cook and stir for 3 minutes. Stir corn mixture into onion mixture in skillet. Place chops on corn mixture. Bring to boiling; reduce heat. Simmer, covered, for 10 to 12 minutes or until pork juices run clear (160°F).

3. To serve, remove chops from skillet. Stir snipped cilantro into corn mixture in skillet; serve corn mixture with chops.

Makes 4 servings

PER SERVING: 330 cal., 11 g total fat (3 g sat. fat), 93 mg chol., 360 mg sodium, 18 g carbo., 2 g fiber, 40 g pro.

40
MINUTES

FISH ENCHILADA STACKS

START TO FINISH: *40 minutes*

- **12 ounces fresh or frozen skinless fish fillets, ½ inch thick**
- **1 tablespoon olive oil**
- **1 tablespoon lime juice**
- **¼ teaspoon ground cumin**
- **⅛ teaspoon garlic powder**
- **2 10-ounce cans enchilada sauce**
- **1 15-ounce can refried black beans**
- **12 5- to 6-inch corn tortillas**
- **2 cups shredded cheddar cheese (8 ounces)**
- **¼ cup chopped green onions**
- **¼ cup chopped pitted ripe olives**

SHOPPING LIST

12 ounces fresh or frozen fish fillets
1 lime
2 10-ounce cans enchilada sauce
1 15-ounce can refried black beans
1 package 5- to 6- inch corn tortillas
1 8-ounce package shredded cheddar cheese
1 bunch green onions
1 2.25-ounce can sliced ripe olives

PANTRY LIST

Olive oil
Ground cumin
Garlic powder

1. Thaw fish, if frozen. Preheat oven to 425°F. Rinse fish; pat dry with paper towels. Cut fish crosswise into ¾-inch slices. Place fish in a single layer in a greased shallow baking pan. In a small bowl stir together olive oil, lime juice, cumin, and garlic powder. Brush over fish. Bake for 4 to 6 minutes or until fish flakes when tested with a fork. Flake fish and set aside. Reduce oven temperature to 350°F.

2. Meanwhile, in a medium skillet warm enchilada sauce over low heat; keep warm. In a small saucepan warm beans over low heat, stirring until smooth; remove from heat.

3. Dip 1 tortilla in warm sauce. Place tortilla in a greased 15×10×1-inch baking pan. Repeat with 3 more tortillas, spacing tortillas evenly in pan. Top tortillas with half of the beans, half of the fish, and ⅔ cup of the cheese. Top with 4 more dipped tortillas, remaining beans and fish, and ⅔ cup of the cheese. Dip remaining tortillas and top stacks. Sprinkle with remaining ⅔ cup cheese.

4. Bake, uncovered, for 8 to 10 minutes or until cheese melts and stacks are heated through. Transfer stacks to serving plates. Spoon any remaining warm sauce over stacks. Sprinkle with green onions and olives.

Makes 4 servings

PER SERVING: 640 cal., 29 g total fat (13 g sat. fat), 96 mg chol., 1,841 mg sodium, 58 g carbo., 11 g fiber, 39 g pro.

40
MINUTES

ITALIAN FISH FINGERS

START TO FINISH: *40 minutes*

- **1 pound fresh or frozen firm white fish fillets, ½ to ¾ inch thick**
- **Salt and ground black pepper**
- **½ cup all-purpose flour**
- **3 eggs, lightly beaten**
- **⅔ cup Italian seasoned fine dry bread crumbs**
- **⅓ cup grated Parmesan cheese**
- **⅓ cup olive oil**
- **1 cup purchased marinara sauce**

SHOPPING LIST

1 pound fresh or frozen firm white fish fillets, ½ to ¾ inch thick

1 9-ounce package Italian seasoned fine dry bread crumbs

1 8-ounce package grated Parmesan cheese

1 14-ounce jar marinara sauce

PANTRY LIST

Salt

Ground black pepper

All-purpose flour

Eggs

Olive oil

1. Thaw fish, if frozen. Rinse fish; pat dry with paper towels. Cut fish into 3×1-inch pieces. Sprinkle with salt and pepper.

2. Place flour in a shallow dish. Place eggs in a second shallow dish. In a third shallow dish combine bread crumbs and Parmesan cheese. Dip fish pieces in flour; shake off excess. Dip in egg, then dip in crumb mixture to coat.

3. In a large skillet cook fish pieces, one-fourth at a time, in hot oil over medium heat for 5 minutes or until golden brown and fish flakes when tested with a fork, turning to brown on all sides. Drain on paper towels. Keep cooked fish warm in a 200°F oven while cooking remaining fish.

4. Meanwhile, in a small saucepan cook marinara sauce over medium heat until heated through. Serve fish fingers with marinara sauce for dipping.

Makes 4 servings

PER SERVING: 505 cal., 26 g total fat (4 g sat. fat), 213 mg chol., 1,159 mg sodium, 33 g carbo., 2 g fiber, 32 g pro.

Baking Option: Preheat oven to 450°F. Line a baking sheet with foil. Lightly coat the foil with olive oil cooking spray. Place the coated fish fingers on the prepared baking sheet. Coat fish pieces well with olive oil cooking spray. Bake for 13 to 15 minutes or until golden brown and fish flakes easily when tested with a fork, turning once halfway through baking.

40
MINUTES

GROUPER WITH TROPICAL SALSA

START TO FINISH: *35 minutes*

- **4** **6- to 8-ounce fresh or frozen grouper or catfish fillets**
- **½** **cup all-purpose flour**
- **½** **cup finely chopped pistachio nuts or almonds**
- **1** **teaspoon ground black pepper**
- **½** **teaspoon salt**
- **½** **teaspoon dried tarragon, crushed**
- **½** **teaspoon dried basil, crushed**
- **¼** **cup milk**
- **¼** **cup lemon-flavor olive oil or olive oil**
- **1** **15.25-ounce can tropical fruit salad, drained and coarsely chopped**
- **1** **tablespoon white balsamic vinegar**
- **1** **tablespoon lime juice**
- **1** **tablespoon snipped fresh cilantro**

1. Thaw fish, if frozen. Preheat oven to 450°F. Grease a 15×10×1-inch baking pan; set aside. Rinse fish; pat dry with paper towels.

2. In a shallow dish combine flour, pistachios, pepper, salt, tarragon, and basil. Place milk in another shallow dish. Dip fish in milk, then coat with flour mixture, patting flour mixture onto fish, if necessary. Place in a single layer in prepared pan. Drizzle fish with oil. Bake for 12 to 15 minutes or until fish flakes when tested with a fork.

3. Meanwhile, for salsa, in a small bowl combine tropical fruit salad, vinegar, lime juice, and cilantro. Serve salsa with fish.

Makes 4 servings

PER SERVING: 490 cal., 23 g total fat (3 g sat. fat), 64 mg chol., 405 mg sodium, 33 g carbo., 3 g fiber, 39 g pro.

SHOPPING LIST

4 6-ounce fresh or frozen grouper fillets

1 2.25-ounce package pistachio nuts

1 small container dried tarragon

1 small bottle lemon-flavor olive oil

1 15.25-ounce can tropical fruit salad

1 8-ounce bottle white balsamic vinegar

1 lime

1 bunch fresh cilantro

PANTRY LIST

All-purpose flour

Ground black pepper

Salt

Dried basil

Milk

40
MINUTES

SALMON WITH ASPARAGUS AND MUSHROOMS

START TO FINISH: *40 minutes*

- **4 fresh or frozen skinless salmon fillets, about 1 inch thick (about 1 pound total)**
- **Salt and ground black pepper**
- **2 cups sliced fresh mushrooms**
- **2 tablespoons olive oil**
- **1 cup chopped onion (1 large)**
- **6 cloves garlic, minced**
- **1 tablespoon snipped fresh thyme**
- **1 cup dry white wine or chicken broth**
- **1 cup clam juice or chicken broth**
- **2 cups 1½-inch pieces asparagus**
- **1 cup cherry tomatoes, halved**
- **1 tablespoon snipped fresh (flat-leaf) parsley**
- **1 teaspoon lemon juice**

1. Thaw fish, if frozen. Rinse fish; pat dry with paper towels. Season fish with salt and pepper. Set aside.

2. In a large skillet cook mushrooms in 1 tablespoon hot oil over medium heat about 5 minutes or until golden brown. Add onion, garlic, and thyme; cook until mushrooms are tender. Add wine. Bring to boiling; reduce heat. Simmer, uncovered, about 15 minutes or until liquid is reduced to ¼ cup.

3. Add clam juice. Return to boiling; reduce heat. Simmer, uncovered, 15 minutes more or until liquid is reduced to ¾ cup. Add asparagus. Cook, covered, 3 minutes or until asparagus is crisp-tender. Stir in tomatoes, parsley, and lemon juice. Season with salt and pepper. Transfer to a platter and keep warm.

4. In the same skillet cook salmon in remaining 1 tablespoon hot oil over medium heat for 4 to 6 minutes per ½-inch thickness of salmon or until salmon flakes when tested with a fork, turning once. Serve salmon over vegetable mixture.

Makes 4 servings

PER SERVING: 371 cal., 20 g total fat (4 g sat. fat), 67 mg chol., 289 mg sodium, 12 g carbo., 3 g fiber, 28 g pro.

SHOPPING LIST

4 fresh or frozen skinless salmon fillets
1 8-ounce package sliced fresh mushrooms
1 large onion
1 package fresh thyme
1 bottle dry white wine
1 8-ounce bottle clam juice
1 pound fresh asparagus
1 pint cherry tomatoes
1 bunch fresh parsley
1 lemon

PANTRY LIST

Salt
Ground black pepper
Olive oil
Garlic

40
MINUTES

BASIL-LIME SALMON

START TO FINISH: *40 minutes*

- **4** **5- to 6-ounce fresh or frozen salmon or halibut steaks, cut 1 inch thick**
- **Salt and ground black pepper**
- **⅓** **cup finely chopped fresh basil**
- **3** **tablespoons olive oil**
- **1** **tablespoon fresh lime juice**
- **1** **clove garlic, minced**
- **¼** **teaspoon salt**
- **⅛** **teaspoon cayenne pepper**
- **Nonstick cooking spray**
- **Lime wedges**

SHOPPING LIST

4 5- to 6-ounce fresh or frozen salmon steaks, 1 inch thick

1 bunch fresh basil

2 limes

PANTRY LIST

Salt

Ground black pepper

Olive oil

Garlic

Cayenne pepper

Nonstick cooking spray

1. Thaw fish, if frozen. Rinse fish; pat dry with paper towels. Sprinkle lightly with salt and black pepper. Set aside.

2. In a small bowl whisk together basil, olive oil, lime juice, garlic, salt, and cayenne pepper until well combined. Place fish in a shallow dish. Pour basil mixture over fish, turning to coat. Cover and refrigerate for 20 minutes.

3. Lightly coat the unheated rack of a broiler pan with cooking spray. Place fish on the broiler pan. Broil 4 to 5 inches from the heat for 8 to 12 minutes or until fish flakes when tested with a fork, turning once halfway through broiling. Serve fish with lime wedges.

Makes 4 servings

PER SERVING: 355 cal., 26 g total fat (5 g sat. fat), 84 mg chol., 375 mg sodium, 2 g carbo., 0 g fiber, 28 g pro.

40
MINUTES

ASIAN SALMON BURGERS

START TO FINISH: *40 minutes*

- **1 egg, lightly beaten**
- **¼ cup milk**
- **½ cup sliced green onions (4)**
- **1 teaspoon five-spice powder**
- **1 14.75-ounce can salmon, drained, flaked, and skin and bones removed**
- **¼ cup panko (Japanese-style bread crumbs)**
- **1 tablespoon cooking oil**
- **3 cups packaged shredded cabbage and carrot (coleslaw mix)**
- **1 medium red sweet pepper, cut into bite-size strips**
- **2 tablespoons chopped fresh cilantro**
- **⅓ cup bottled Asian toasted sesame salad dressing**
- **4 hamburger buns, split and toasted**

1. In a medium bowl combine egg, milk, half of the green onions, and the five-spice powder. Add salmon and bread crumbs; mix well. Form mixture into four ¾-inch-thick patties. In a large skillet cook patties in hot oil over medium heat about 6 minutes or until golden brown and heated through (160°F), turning once.

2. In a medium bowl combine cabbage, sweet pepper, remaining green onions, and cilantro. Add salad dressing; toss to mix. Place salmon patties in buns; top patties with some of the cabbage mixture. Serve remaining cabbage mixture on the side.

Makes 4 servings

PER SERVING: 435 cal., 19 g total fat (4 g sat. fat), 112 mg chol., 1,036 mg sodium, 35 g carbo., 3 g fiber, 28 g pro.

SHOPPING LIST

1 bunch green onions

1 small jar five-spice powder

1 14.75-ounce can salmon

1 8-ounce package panko (Japanese-style bread crumbs)

1 16-ounce package shredded cabbage and carrot (coleslaw mix)

1 medium red sweet pepper

1 bunch cilantro

1 16-ounce bottle Asian toasted sesame salad dressing

1 package hamburger buns

PANTRY LIST

Egg

Milk

Cooking oil

40
MINUTES

SHRIMP TACOS

START TO FINISH: *35 minutes*

- **8 6-inch corn tortillas**
- **1½ cups chopped, seeded tomato**
- **1 cup chopped, seeded cucumber**
- **⅓ cup thinly sliced green onions**
- **¼ cup snipped fresh cilantro**
- **3 tablespoons lime juice**
- **¼ teaspoon salt**
- **8 ounces fresh green beans, trimmed and halved crosswise**
- **1 teaspoon Jamaican jerk seasoning**
- **1 pound medium to large shrimp in shells, peeled and deveined**
- **1 tablespoon olive oil**

1. Preheat oven to 350°F. Wrap tortillas in heavy foil. Heat tortillas in oven for 10 minutes. Meanwhile, for salsa, in a medium bowl combine tomato, cucumber, green onions, cilantro, lime juice, and salt; set aside.

2. In a bowl toss beans with ½ teaspoon of the seasoning. In another bowl toss shrimp with remaining ½ teaspoon seasoning. In a large skillet cook and stir green beans in hot oil over medium-high heat for 3 minutes. Add shrimp to skillet; cook and stir for 2 to 3 minutes more or until shrimp are opaque.

3. Fill each warm tortilla with about ⅓ cup of the shrimp mixture. Serve with salsa.

Makes 4 servings

PER SERVING: 274 cal., 7 g total fat (1 g sat. fat), 129 mg chol., 381 mg sodium, 33 g carbo., 7 g fiber, 22 g pro.

SHOPPING LIST

1 package 6-inch corn tortillas
2 medium tomatoes
1 medium cucumber
1 bunch green onions
1 bunch fresh cilantro
1 lime
8 ounces fresh green beans
1 small container Jamaican jerk seasoning
1 pound medium shrimp in shells

PANTRY LIST

Salt
Olive oil

40 MINUTES

SESAME SHRIMP STIR-FRY

START TO FINISH: *40 minutes*

- **6 ounces fresh or frozen large shrimp in shells**
- **¼ cup unsweetened apple juice**
- **1 teaspoon dry Chinese-style hot mustard**
- **1 teaspoon reduced-sodium soy sauce**
- **1 teaspoon grated fresh ginger**
- **Nonstick cooking spray**
- **1 small red sweet pepper, seeded and cut into ½-inch pieces**
- **2 ounces small fresh mushrooms, halved**
- **2 green onions, chopped**
- **½ cup fresh sugar snap peas, trimmed and cut in half crosswise**
- **1 medium carrot, cut into thin bite-size strips**
- **¼ cup thinly sliced celery**
- **1 clove garlic, minced**
- **1 teaspoon sesame seeds, toasted**

1. Thaw shrimp, if frozen. Peel and devein shrimp. Rinse shrimp; pat dry with paper towels. Cut shrimp in half lengthwise; set aside. In a small bowl combine apple juice, mustard, soy sauce, and ginger; set aside.

2. Coat a large nonstick skillet with cooking spray. Heat skillet over medium-high heat. Cook sweet pepper, mushrooms, and green onions in skillet for 2 to 4 minutes or until mushrooms are tender, stirring frequently. Stir in sugar snap peas, carrot, celery, and garlic. Cook and stir for 2 to 4 minutes more or until the peas are crisp-tender. Remove vegetables from skillet.

3. Add shrimp to skillet; cook and stir for 1 to 2 minutes or until the shrimp are opaque. Return vegetables to skillet. Stir to combine. Add apple juice mixture to skillet. Cook and stir until heated through. Sprinkle with sesame seeds.

Makes 2 servings

PER SERVING: 164 cal., 3 g total fat (0 g sat. fat), 129 mg chol., 261 mg sodium, 15 g carbo., 3 g fiber, 21 g pro.

SHOPPING LIST

6 ounces fresh or frozen large shrimp in shells

1 5-ounce can unsweetened apple juice

1 small container dry Chinese-style hot mustard

1 5-ounce bottle reduced-sodium soy sauce

1 piece fresh ginger

1 small red sweet pepper

1 8-ounce package fresh mushrooms

1 bunch green onions

2 ounces fresh sugar snap peas

1 package carrots

1 bunch celery

1 small container sesame seeds

PANTRY LIST

Nonstick cooking spray

Garlic

40 MINUTES

PASTA WITH MUSHROOMS AND AGED JACK CHEESE

START TO FINISH: *35 minutes*

- **8 ounces dried penne or campanelle**
- **1 tablespoon butter**
- **1 large sweet onion, cut into thin wedges**
- **4 cloves garlic, minced**
- **2 tablespoons butter**
- **3 cups sliced fresh mushrooms**
- **½ cup whipping cream**
- **¼ cup chicken broth**
- **4 ounces aged (dry) Jack cheese, finely shredded (1 cup firmly packed)**
- **Salt and freshly ground black pepper**
- **Fresh thyme (optional)**

SHOPPING LIST

1 16-ounce package dried penne
1 large sweet onion
2 8-ounce packages sliced fresh mushrooms
1 8-ounce carton whipping cream
1 14-ounce can chicken broth
4 ounces aged Jack cheese

PANTRY LIST

Butter
Garlic
Salt
Black pepper

1. In a large saucepan cook pasta according to package directions. Drain; return to saucepan. Stir in 1 tablespoon butter. Cover and keep warm.

2. In a large skillet cook and stir onion and garlic in 2 tablespoons hot butter over medium heat for 4 to 5 minutes or until tender. Stir in mushrooms; cook 3 minutes more or until tender.

3. Meanwhile, in a small saucepan heat whipping cream and broth over medium heat just to boiling. Reduce heat to low; stir in cheese. Continue stirring until cheese nearly melts. Add mushroom mixture and cream mixture to pasta. Toss to combine; heat through. Season to taste with salt and pepper. If desired, sprinkle with thyme.

Makes 4 servings

PER SERVING: 586 cal., 36 g total fat (18 g sat. fat), 76 mg chol., 352 mg sodium, 50 g carbo., 4 g fiber, 19 g pro.

40
MINUTES

STUFFED SPINACH PIZZA

START TO FINISH: *40 minutes*

- **1 6-ounce package fresh spinach leaves, coarsely chopped (6 cups)**
- **2 cups shredded mozzarella cheese (8 ounces)**
- **1 16-ounce jar pizza sauce**
- **1 teaspoon bottled hot pepper sauce (optional)**
- **2 13.8-ounce cans refrigerated pizza dough**
- **6 ounces sliced provolone cheese**
- **¼ cup shredded Parmesan cheese**

SHOPPING LIST

1 6-ounce package baby spinach

1 8-ounce package shredded mozzarella cheese

1 16-ounce jar pizza sauce

2 13.8-ounce packages refrigerated pizza dough

1 6-ounce package sliced provolone cheese

1 4-ounce package shredded Parmesan cheese

PANTRY LIST

Bottled hot pepper sauce

1. Preheat oven to 450°F. In a very large bowl combine spinach, mozzarella, 1 cup pizza sauce, and, if desired, hot pepper sauce. Set aside.

2. Grease a 13×9×2-inch baking pan. On a lightly floured surface, roll 1 pizza crust into a 17×13-inch rectangle. Place in pan, pressing crust over the bottom and up the sides. Line bottom of crust with provolone cheese slices. Spread spinach mixture over provolone. On the lightly floured surface, roll second crust into a 13×9-inch rectangle. Place over spinach mixture. Pinch edges of crusts together to seal. Prick top of crust all over with a fork.

3. Bake for 20 minutes or until crust is deep golden brown. Remove pizza from oven. Sprinkle with Parmesan cheese. Let stand a few minutes to melt cheese. Heat remaining pizza sauce and pass with pizza.

Makes 6 to 8 servings

PER SERVING: 539 cal., 23 g total fat (11 g sat. fat), 44 mg chol., 1,139 mg sodium, 58 g carbo., 4 g fiber, 27 g pro.

40
MINUTES

PUMPKIN-BEAN BURRITOS

START TO FINISH: *40 minutes*

- **6 10-inch flour tortillas**
- **1 15-ounce can pumpkin**
- **1 15-ounce can black beans, rinsed and drained**
- **1 8.8-ounce package cooked Spanish-style rice**
- **¼ cup sliced green onions (2)**
- **1 tablespoon Mexican seasoning**
- **¼ teaspoon salt**
- **1½ cups shredded Mexican-style four-cheese blend**
- **Purchased salsa (optional)**

SHOPPING LIST

1 package 10-inch flour tortillas
1 15-ounce can pumpkin
1 15-ounce can black beans
1 8.8-ounce package cooked Spanish-style rice
1 bunch green onions
1 small container Mexican seasoning
1 8-ounce package shredded Mexican cheese blend

PANTRY LIST

Salt

1. Preheat oven to 350°F. Stack tortillas; wrap in foil. Bake for 10 minutes or until warm. (Or wrap in microwave-safe paper towels; microwave on 100% power (high), for 1 minute or until warm.) Meanwhile, in a large bowl stir together pumpkin, beans, rice, green onions, Mexican seasoning, and salt.

2. Spoon about ½ cup pumpkin mixture onto each tortilla just below the center. Top with cheese. Fold bottom edge of each tortilla up and over filling. Fold opposite sides in and over filling. Roll up from the bottom.

3. Arrange burritos, seam sides down, on a baking sheet. Bake about 20 minutes or until light brown and heated through. If desired, serve burritos with salsa.

Makes 6 servings

PER SERVING: 474 cal., 15 g total fat (7 g sat. fat), 25 mg chol., 1,149 mg sodium, 68 g carbo., 8 g fiber, 17 g pro.

40
MINUTES

VEGGIE JUMBLE STEW

START TO FINISH: *40 minutes*

- **2 tablespoons olive oil**
- **3 tablespoons all-purpose flour**
- **¼ teaspoon salt**
- **¼ teaspoon ground black pepper**
- **1 pound tiny new potatoes, halved**
- **1 8- to 10-ounce package Brussels sprouts**
- **1½ cups packaged peeled baby carrots**
- **1 cup frozen small whole onions**
- **2 stalks celery, cut into ½-inch pieces**
- **1½ teaspoons bottled minced garlic**
- **1 14-ounce can reduced-sodium chicken broth or vegetable broth**
- **1½ cups apple cider**
- **1 9-ounce package frozen cut green beans**
- **1 1-pound loaf white or wheat bread, cut into 12 slices and toasted**
- **3 ounces thinly sliced white cheddar cheese**

1. In a 4-quart Dutch oven or large pot heat oil over medium heat. Stir in flour, salt, and pepper; cook and stir for 2 minutes. Add potatoes, Brussels sprouts, carrots, onions, celery, and garlic. Cook and stir for 5 minutes more.

2. Stir in broth and cider. Bring to boiling; reduce heat. Simmer, uncovered, for 10 minutes. Add green beans. Simmer 10 minutes more or until vegetables are tender.

3. Place bread in bowls. Top with stew and cheese.

Makes 6 servings

PER SERVING: 461 cal., 12 g total fat (4 g sat. fat), 16 mg chol., 818 mg sodium, 72 g carbo., 7 g fiber, 15 g pro.

SHOPPING LIST

1 pound tiny new potatoes
1 8-ounce package Brussels sprouts
1 16-ounce package fresh baby carrots
1 16-ounce package frozen small whole onions
1 bunch celery
1 14-ounce can reduced-sodium chicken broth
1 32-ounce bottle apple cider
1 9-ounce package frozen cut green beans
1 1-pound loaf white bread
3 ounces thinly sliced white cheddar cheese

PANTRY LIST

Olive oil
All-purpose flour
Salt
Ground black pepper
Bottled minced garlic

PASTA WITH TOMATOES, page 204

SIDES & DESSERTS

15
MINUTES

SNOW PEAS AND TOMATOES

START TO FINISH: *15 minutes*

- **1 large shallot, sliced, or ½ cup thinly sliced red onion or green onions**
- **2 teaspoons cooking oil**
- **¼ teaspoon toasted sesame oil (optional)**
- **2 teaspoons sesame seeds**
- **2 6-ounce packages frozen snow peas**
- **2 tablespoons bottled teriyaki sauce**
- **½ cup grape, cherry, and/or pear-shape red and/or yellow tomatoes, halved**

1. In a large skillet cook shallot in hot cooking and sesame oil (if using) over medium heat until tender. Add sesame seeds. Cook and stir for 1 minute more or until seeds are lightly toasted.

2. Add snow peas and teriyaki sauce. Cook and stir for 2 to 3 minutes or until snow peas are crisp-tender. Stir in tomatoes; cook for 1 minute more.

Makes 6 servings

PER SERVING: 59 cal., 2 g total fat (0 g sat. fat), 0 mg chol., 211 mg sodium, 9 g carbo., 2 g fiber, 3 g pro.

SHOPPING LIST
1 large shallot
1 small container sesame seeds
2 6-ounce packages frozen snow peas
1 8-ounce bottle teriyaki sauce
1 pint grape tomatoes

PANTRY LIST
Cooking oil

15 MINUTES

ASPARAGUS WITH ALMOND SAUCE

START TO FINISH: *15 minutes*

- **1 pound fresh asparagus, trimmed**
- **2 tablespoons sliced almonds**
- **1 tablespoon butter**
- **½ cup chicken broth**
- **1 teaspoon cornstarch**
- **2 teaspoons lemon juice**
- **Dash ground black pepper**

1. In a large saucepan cook asparagus, covered, in boiling lightly salted water for 3 to 5 minutes or until crisp-tender. Drain well; transfer to a serving platter. Keep warm.

2. Meanwhile, for sauce, in a large skillet cook and stir almonds in hot butter over medium heat for 2 to 3 minutes or until golden. In a small bowl stir together broth, cornstarch, lemon juice, and pepper; add to skillet. Cook and stir until thick and bubbly. Cook and stir 1 minute more. Spoon sauce over asparagus.

Makes 4 servings

PER SERVING: 76 cal., 5 g total fat (2 g sat. fat), 8 mg chol., 143 mg sodium, 6 g carbo., 3 g fiber, 3 g pro.

SHOPPING LIST

1 pound fresh asparagus
1 2.25-ounce package sliced almonds
1 14-ounce can chicken broth
1 lemon

PANTRY LIST

Butter
Cornstarch
Ground black pepper

15
MINUTES

ORANGE-GLAZED BABY CARROTS

START TO FINISH: *15 minutes*

2 cups packaged peeled fresh baby carrots
2 tablespoons orange marmalade
1 tablespoon butter

1. In a medium saucepan cook carrots, covered, in lightly salted boiling water for 5 minutes. Drain; set aside.

2. In the same saucepan cook and stir drained carrots and marmalade in hot butter over medium heat for 2 to 3 minutes or until carrots are tender and glazed.

Makes 4 servings

PER SERVING: 77 cal., 3 g total fat (2 g sat. fat), 8 mg chol., 57 mg sodium, 13 g carbo., 2 g fiber, 1 g pro.

SHOPPING LIST
1 16-ounce package fresh baby carrots
1 10-ounce jar orange marmalade

PANTRY LIST
Butter

15
MINUTES

SKILLET SCALLOPED CORN

START TO FINISH: *15 minutes*

- **2 teaspoons butter**
- **½ cup crushed rich round, wheat, or rye crackers**
- **1 11-ounce can whole kernel corn with sweet peppers, drained**
- **1 7- to 8.75-ounce can whole kernel corn with sweet peppers, whole kernel corn, or white corn, drained**
- **2 1-ounce slices process Swiss cheese, torn**
- **⅓ cup milk**
- **⅛ teaspoon onion powder**
- **Dash ground black pepper**

1. For topping, in a large skillet melt butter over medium heat. Add 2 tablespoons of the crushed crackers. Cook and stir until light brown; remove and set aside.

2. In the same skillet combine remaining crushed crackers, both kinds of corn, cheese, milk, onion powder, and pepper. Cook, stirring frequently, until cheese melts. Transfer to a serving dish; sprinkle with reserved topping.

Makes 4 servings

PER SERVING: 183 cal., 9 g total fat (4 g sat. fat), 18 mg chol., 704 mg sodium, 19 g carbo., 2 g fiber, 6 g pro.

SHOPPING LIST

1 8-ounce package rich round crackers
1 11-ounce can whole kernel corn with sweet peppers
1 7-ounce can whole kernel corn with sweet peppers
1 8-ounce packaged sliced process Swiss cheese
1 small container onion powder

PANTRY LIST

Butter
Milk
Ground black pepper

15
MINUTES

MASHED POTATOES WITH THE WORKS

START TO FINISH: *10 minutes*

- **1 24-ounce package refrigerated mashed potatoes**
- **½ cup dairy sour cream**
- **2 tablespoons snipped fresh chives**
- **4 slices packaged ready-to-serve cooked bacon, torn into bite-size pieces**
- **½ cup shredded cheddar cheese**

1. Heat potatoes according to package directions. (If using microwave directions, transfer potatoes to a medium bowl.) Stir in sour cream, chives, and bacon. Top each serving with cheese.

Makes 4 servings

PER SERVING: 284 cal., 15 g total fat (7 g sat. fat), 34 mg chol., 547 mg sodium, 24 g carbo., 1 g fiber, 11 g pro.

SHOPPING LIST

1 24-ounce package refrigerated mashed potatoes
1 8-ounce carton dairy sour cream
1 bunch fresh chives
1 2.1-ounce package ready-to-serve cooked bacon
1 8-ounce package shredded cheddar cheese

15
MINUTES

ZESTY MASHED POTATOES

START TO FINISH: *15 minutes*

- **½ cup chopped red onion and/or sliced green onions**
- **1 tablespoon butter**
- **1½ teaspoons Jamaican jerk seasoning**
- **¼ teaspoon ground black pepper**
- **2 20-ounce packages refrigerated mashed potatoes**
- **1 8-ounce carton dairy sour cream**

1. In a large saucepan cook onion in hot butter over medium heat for 3 to 4 minutes or until tender. Stir in jerk seasoning and pepper. Stir in mashed potatoes and sour cream. Cook until heated through, stirring frequently.

Makes 8 servings

PER SERVING: 189 cal., 10 g total fat (5 g sat. fat), 17 mg chol., 300 mg sodium, 21 g carbo., 1 g fiber, 4 g pro.

SHOPPING LIST

1 medium red onion

1 small container Jamaican jerk seasoning

2 20-ounce packages refrigerated mashed potatoes

1 8-ounce carton dairy sour cream

PANTRY LIST

Butter

Ground black pepper

15
MINUTES

MIXED GREENS SALAD WITH PEARS

START TO FINISH: *15 minutes*

- **1 5-ounce bag spring mixed salad greens**
- **2 medium fresh pears, cored and sliced**
- **2 ounces Gruyère cheese, cubed**
- **White Wine Vinaigrette or ¼ cup bottled red wine vinaigrette plus 2 teaspoons honey**
- **Thin fresh pear slices (optional)**

1. In a large bowl combine greens, pears, and cheese. Drizzle vinaigrette over greens mixture and toss to coat. If desired, garnish with pear slices.

Makes 6 servings

WHITE WINE VINAIGRETTE: In a screw-top jar combine 3 tablespoons salad oil; 2 tablespoons white wine vinegar; 1 tablespoon honey; ¼ teaspoon dried basil or oregano, crushed; ⅛ teaspoon salt; ⅛ teaspoon dry mustard; and ⅛ teaspoon ground black pepper. Cover and shake to combine.

PER SERVING: 148 cal., 10 g total fat (3 g sat. fat), 10 mg chol., 85 mg sodium, 12 g carbo., 2 g fiber, 3 g pro.

SHOPPING LIST

1 5-ounce bag spring mixed salad greens
2 medium pears
2 ounces Gruyère cheese
1 8-ounce bottle white wine vinegar
1 small container dry mustard

PANTRY LIST

Salad oil
Honey
Dried basil
Salt
Ground black pepper

15
MINUTES

MEDITERRANEAN SALAD

START TO FINISH: *10 minutes*

- **1 6.5-ounce jar marinated artichoke hearts, drained**
- **1 15-ounce can three-bean salad, drained**
- **1 large tomato, seeded and chopped**
- **1 tablespoon snipped fresh basil or ½ teaspoon dried basil, crushed**
- **¼ cup Italian salad dressing**
- **Lettuce leaves (optional)**

1. Halve any large artichoke hearts. In a medium bowl combine artichoke hearts, three-bean salad, tomato, and basil. Drizzle Italian dressing over bean mixture; toss gently to coat. If desired, serve on lettuce leaves.

Makes 6 servings

PER SERVING: 109 cal., 5 g total fat (0 g sat. fat), 0 mg chol., 538 mg sodium, 16 g carbo., 3 g fiber, 3 g pro.

SHOPPING LIST

1 6.5-ounce jar marinated artichoke hearts
1 15-ounce can three-bean salad
1 large tomato
1 package fresh basil
1 8-ounce bottle Italian salad dressing

15
MINUTES

BLT COLESLAW

START TO FINISH: *15 minutes*

- **1** **16-ounce package shredded cabbage with carrot (coleslaw mix)**
- **6** **slices packaged ready-to-serve cooked bacon, torn into bite-size pieces**
- **1** **pint grape or cherry tomatoes, halved**
- **½** **cup bottled ranch salad dressing**

1. In a large bowl combine coleslaw mix, bacon, tomatoes, and salad dressing. Toss to coat.

Makes 8 to 10 servings

PER SERVING: 110 cal., 9 g total fat (2 g sat. fat), 8 mg chol., 201 mg sodium, 6 g carbo., 2 g fiber, 3 g pro.

SHOPPING LIST

1 16-ounce package shredded cabbage with carrot (coleslaw mix)

1 2.1-ounce package ready-to-serve cooked bacon

1 pint grape tomatoes

1 8-ounce bottle ranch salad dressing

15
MINUTES

BROCCOLI SLAW

START TO FINISH: *10 minutes*

- **⅓ cup mayonnaise or salad dressing**
- **2 tablespoons cider vinegar**
- **1 green onion, finely chopped (2 tablespoons)**
- **1½ teaspoons sugar**
- **¾ teaspoon salt**
- **5 cups shredded broccoli (broccoli slaw mix) or shredded cabbage with carrot (coleslaw mix)**

1. For dressing, in a salad bowl stir together mayonnaise, vinegar, green onion, sugar, and salt. Add shredded broccoli; toss to coat.

Makes 4 to 5 servings

PER SERVINGS: 172 cal., 15 g total fat (2 g sat. fat), 7 mg chol., 566 mg sodium, 8 g carbo., 3 g fiber, 3 g pro.

SHOPPING LIST

1 bunch green onions

1 12-ounce package shredded broccoli (broccoli slaw mix)

PANTRY LIST

Mayonnaise

Cider vinegar

Sugar

Salt

15
MINUTES

PASTA WITH TOMATOES

START TO FINISH: *15 minutes*

- **2 tablespoons olive oil**
- **½ teaspoon snipped fresh rosemary**
- **1 9-ounce package refrigerated fettuccine***
- **⅔ cup red and/or gold grape tomatoes, teardrop tomatoes, or cherry tomatoes, halved**
- **¼ cup fresh Italian (flat-leaf) parsley leaves**
- **Salt**
- **Coarsely ground black pepper**
- **Grated Parmesan cheese**

SHOPPING LIST

1 package fresh rosemary

1 9-ounce package refrigerated fettuccine

1 pint grape tomatoes

1 bunch fresh Italian (flat-leaf) parsley

1 7-ounce container grated Parmesan cheese

PANTRY LIST

Olive oil

Salt

Black pepper

1. In a small bowl stir together oil and rosemary. Cover and set aside.

2. In a Dutch oven or large saucepan bring 3 quarts salted water to boiling. Cook pasta, uncovered, according to package directions until tender but still firm. Drain pasta; return to pan.

3. Add oil mixture, tomatoes, and parsley to pasta; toss to coat. Season to taste with salt and pepper. Sprinkle with Parmesan cheese.

Makes 4 servings

PER SERVING: 258 cal., 9 g total fat (2 g sat. fat), 43 mg chol., 202 mg sodium, 35 g carbo., 2 g fiber, 10 g pro.

*Note: Snip pasta into shorter lengths, if desired.

15
MINUTES

HEAVENLY COUSCOUS

START TO FINISH: *15 minutes*

- **1 cup couscous**
- **¼ teaspoon salt**
- **1 cup boiling water**
- **¼ cup slivered almonds**
- **1 teaspoon butter**
- **¼ cup snipped dried apricots**
- **½ teaspoon finely shredded orange peel**

1. In a medium bowl combine couscous and salt. Gradually add the boiling water. Let stand about 5 minutes or until liquid is absorbed.

2. Meanwhile, in a small skillet cook and stir almonds in hot butter over medium heat until almonds are light golden brown. Remove almonds from skillet to cool. Fluff couscous with a fork. Add apricots, orange peel, and toasted almonds to couscous. Fluff again. Serve immediately.

Makes 4 servings

PER SERVING: 250 cal., 5 g total fat (1 g sat. fat), 2 mg chol., 163 mg sodium, 42 g carbo., 4 g fiber, 8 g pro.

SHOPPING LIST

1 12-ounce package couscous

1 2.25-ounce package slivered almonds

1 3-ounce package dried apricots

1 orange

PANTRY LIST

Salt

Butter

15
MINUTES

QUICK BROWNIE SURPRISE

START TO FINISH: *10 minutes*

- **4** **purchased brownies (each about 3×2 inches)**
- **1** **15.10- to 16-ounce carton cherry-chocolate ice cream**
- **¼** **cup dried cherries**
- **¼** **cup chopped mixed nuts or nut topping**
- **2** **tablespoons chocolate-flavor syrup**

1. Place 1 brownie in each of 4 dessert bowls. Top with a scoop of ice cream. Sprinkle with cherries and nuts. Drizzle with syrup.

Makes 4 servings

PER SERVING: 660 cal., 35 g total fat (17 g sat. fat), 81 mg chol., 255 mg sodium, 81 g carbo., 3 g fiber, 9 g pro.

SHOPPING LIST

4 bakery brownies

1 15.10- to 16-ounce carton cherry-chocolate ice cream

1 3-ounce package dried tart red cherries

1 small container mixed nuts

1 24-ounce bottle chocolate-flavor syrup

15
MINUTES

QUICK APPLE CRISP

START TO FINISH: *15 minutes*

- **1 21-ounce can apple pie filling**
- **¼ cup dried cranberries**
- **¼ teaspoon ground ginger or ground cinnamon**
- **¼ teaspoon vanilla**
- **1 cup granola**
- **1 pint vanilla ice cream**

1. In a medium saucepan combine pie filling, cranberries, and ginger; heat through, stirring occasionally. Remove from heat; stir in vanilla. Spoon into 4 bowls. Top with granola and ice cream.

Makes 4 servings

PER SERVING: 507 cal., 15 g total fat (8 g sat. fat), 68 mg chol., 113 mg sodium, 88 g carbo., 6 g fiber, 9 g pro.

SHOPPING LIST

1 21-ounce can apple pie filling
1 3-ounce package dried cranberries
1 small container ground ginger
1 1-ounce bottle vanilla
1 16-ounce box granola cereal
1 pint vanilla ice cream

15
MINUTES

BITTERSWEET CHOCOLATE-ORANGE FONDUE

START TO FINISH: *15 minutes*

- **6 ounces bittersweet chocolate, coarsely chopped**
- **¾ cup half-and-half or light cream**
- **⅓ cup sugar**
- **¼ cup orange liqueur or orange juice**
- **2 tablespoons honey**
- **Dippers (such as dried fruits; biscotti cookies; clementines, tangerines, or oranges, peeled and sectioned; pear or apple wedges; whole walnuts, almonds, or pecans)**

1. In a heavy small saucepan melt chocolate over medium-low heat. Whisk in half-and-half until smooth; stir in sugar, orange liqueur, and honey. Cook, stirring constantly, for 4 to 5 minutes or until mixture is slightly thick and sugar dissolves. Transfer to a fondue pot. Keep warm over low heat. Serve with desired dippers.

Makes 8 servings

PER SERVING: 205 cal., 11 g total fat (7 g sat. fat), 9 mg chol., 10 mg sodium, 28 g carbo., 2 g fiber, 2 g pro.

SHOPPING LIST

1 6-ounce package bittersweet baking chocolate

1 8-ounce carton half-and-half

1 small bottle orange liqueur

Desired dippers

PANTRY LIST

Sugar

Honey

15
MINUTES

CINNAMON TOASTED POUND CAKE AND STRAWBERRIES

START TO FINISH: *15 minutes*

- **½ teaspoon ground cinnamon**
- **1 tablespoon sugar**
- **3 cups strawberries, washed and quartered**
- **¼ cup strawberry jam**
- **1 tablespoon lemon juice**
- **1 10.75-ounce frozen pound cake, thawed and cut into 12 slices**
- **2 tablespoons butter, softened**
- **Frozen whipped dessert topping, thawed**

1. In a small bowl stir together cinnamon and sugar. In a large bowl toss together strawberries, jam, lemon juice, and 1 teaspoon of the cinnamon-sugar mixture until berries are well coated.

2. Toast pound cake slices. Spread 1 side of each slice with butter. Sprinkle with remaining cinnamon-sugar mixture. To serve, place 2 pound cake slices on each of 6 plates. Top with strawberries and whipped topping.

Makes 6 servings

PER SERVING: 875 cal., 56 g total fat (31 g sat. fat), 378 mg chol., 540 mg sodium, 135 g carbo., 5 g fiber, 13 g pro.

SHOPPING LIST

1 quart strawberries
1 10-ounce jar strawberry jam
1 lemon
1 10.75-ounce frozen pound cake
1 8-ounce container frozen whipped dessert topping

PANTRY LIST

Sugar
Ground cinnamon
Butter

15
MINUTES

CHOCOLATE-PEANUT BUTTER-ICE CREAM SANDWICHES

START TO FINISH: *15 minutes*

- **1 pint tin roof sundae or other chocolate swirl premium ice cream**
- **8 3½-inch purchased peanut butter cookies**
- **¼ cup miniature semisweet chocolate pieces or crushed chocolate-covered crisp peanut butter candy**

1. Place a scoop of ice cream on the bottoms of 4 cookies. Top with remaining 4 cookies, flat sides down. Press gently to force ice cream to the edges of the cookies. Place chocolate pieces in a shallow dish. Roll edges of ice cream sandwiches in the chocolate pieces to coat. Freeze for 5 minutes or until firm.

Makes 4 servings

PER SERVING: 625 cal., 36 g total fat (17 g sat. fat), 123 mg chol., 312 mg sodium, 65 g carbo., 2 g fiber, 11 g pro.

SHOPPING LIST

1 pint tin roof sundae ice cream

8 bakery peanut butter cookies

1 12-ounce package miniature semisweet chocolate pieces

15
MINUTES

MOCHA MOUSSE CUPS

START TO FINISH: *15 minutes*

- **2** **teaspoons instant espresso powder or 1 tablespoon instant coffee crystals**
- **1** **tablespoon hot water**
- **4** **3.5- to 4-ounce containers chocolate pudding (prepared pudding cups), chilled**
- **½** **of an 8-ounce container frozen whipped dessert topping, thawed**
- **9** **chocolate wafer cookies, coarsely crushed**

1. In a medium bowl stir espresso powder into the hot water until dissolved. Stir in chilled pudding. Fold in whipped topping. Divide half of the pudding mixture among 6 dessert dishes. Sprinkle with half of the coarsely crushed cookies. Repeat layers.

Makes 6 servings

PER SERVING: 187 cal., 7 g total fat (5 g sat. fat), 0 mg chol., 164 mg sodium, 27 g carbo., 0 g fiber, 2 g pro.

SHOPPING LIST

1 2-ounce jar instant espresso powder
4 3.5-ounce containers chocolate pudding
1 8-ounce container frozen whipped dessert topping
1 9-ounce package chocolate wafer cookies

15
MINUTES

TROPICAL BREEZE SUNDAE

START TO FINISH: *15 minutes*

- **1 quart pineapple, lime, or orange sherbet or sorbet**
- **Fresh pineapple, papaya, or mango slices**
- **½ to ¾ cup pineapple ice cream topping**
- **Pressurized whipped dessert topping**

1. Scoop sherbet into 6 dessert dishes. Add fruit slices. Top each serving with a spoonful of ice cream topping and some whipped dessert topping. Serve immediately.

Makes 6 servings

PER SERVING: 282 cal., 0 g total fat (0 g sat. fat), 0 mg chol., 46 mg sodium, 72 g carbo., 0 g fiber, 0 g pro.

SHOPPING LIST

1 quart pineapple sherbet
1 fresh pineapple
1 12-ounce jar pineapple ice cream topping
1 6.5-ounce can pressurized whipped dessert topping

15
MINUTES

GRILLED CHOCOLATE-BANANA SANDWICH

START TO FINISH: *10 minutes*

- **½ of a 3.5-ounce chocolate bar, halved**
- **2 slices white or whole wheat bread**
- **½ of a banana, sliced**
- **1 tablespoon butter**
- **Sifted powdered sugar**

1. Place the chocolate bar on 1 bread slice. Top with the banana slices and remaining slice of bread. In a skillet heat butter over medium-low heat just until it begins to bubble. Add sandwich to skillet, chocolate side down. Cook, covered, about 1½ minutes or until bread is golden brown and toasted. Carefully flip sandwich over and cook until brown. Remove from skillet, slice in half, and dust with powdered sugar. Serve warm.

Makes 1 serving

PER SERVING: 560 cal., 29 g total fat (17 g sat. fat), 42 mg chol., 473 mg sodium, 70 g carbo., 4 g fiber, 11 g pro.

SHOPPING LIST

1 3.5-ounce chocolate bar

2 slices bread

1 banana

PANTRY LIST

Butter

Powdered sugar